ALL TOGETHER NOW:
Museums and Online Collaborative Learning

Crow, William B., 1973-
    All together now : museums and online collaborative learning / by William B. Crow and Herminia Wei-Hsin Din.
        p. cm.
    Includes index.
    ISBN 978-1-933253-61-9 (alk. paper)
    1. Museums--Educational aspects. 2. Web-based instruction. 3. Museums--Information technology. 4. Museum techniques. 5. Museums--Educational aspects--Case studies. 6. Web-based instruction--Case studies. 7. Museums--Information technology--Case studies. 8. Museum techniques--Case studies. I. Din, Herminia Wei-Hsin, 1968- II. Title.

ALL TOGETHER NOW:
Museums and Online Collaborative Learning

BY WILLIAM B. CROW and HERMINIA WEI-HSIN DIN

The AAM Press *of the*

AMERICAN ASSOCIATION OF MUSEUMS
1575 EYE STREET NW, SUITE 400
WASHINGTON DC 20005

TABLE OF CONTENTS

ACKNOWLEDGEMENTS

In 2006 we began our collaborative work in creating online and blended museum-based teacher-training programs. Our work process wasn't always easy, especially given that we were collaborating across many thousands of miles in New York City and Alaska, not to mention working in different institutions. The writing of this book, in fact, was an online collaborative project lasting more than two years. We continue to see great value in the possibilities that online collaboration offers, as we hope this book illustrates, and we are very fortunate to find the collaborative spirit and support of our colleagues, friends, and families.

We are grateful that The AAM Press of the American Association of Museums saw the opportunity to start a dialogue about the possibilities that online learning could offer museums and visitors when the press published our first book in 2009, *Unbound by Place or Time: Museums and Online Learning*. We deeply appreciate the continued support and encouragement that we receive from The AAM Press as we publish this second volume. We thank John Strand, publisher of the AAM Press, and Roger Moyer, head of AAM book sales and distribution, for their wisdom, editorial and design expertise, and encouragement.

We could not have accomplished this book without the expertise and dedication of our colleagues, to whom we extend our sincere gratitude. We would like to express our appreciation to our contributors to each of the case studies, without whom we could not have completed this publication. We also like to thank Educational Enterprise Zone (EEZ) at New York Institute of Technology for their generous tech hosting of all our Elluminate webinar sessions.

Finally, we would like to thank our greatest collaborators, Philip Kain and Darrell Bailey, for their support and encouragement throughout the process.

William B. Crow and Herminia Din

FOREWORD

By Lynda Kennedy

Like many who work with the art and artifacts in cultural institutions, I am a believer in the power of the "real" — the unparalleled experience of standing in front of a work of art or in a historic place. With this world-view, I was not overwhelmed with enthusiasm when collections first were digitized for public consumption. Early attempts to use these digitized collections educationally did not do much to increase my enthusiasm. These early attempts tended to make use of the same engagement techniques used in the halls and galleries of institutions. The digital image would be posted on a website while text alongside it would ask the same sort of questions and give the same sort of information we could have received standing in front of the real thing. Though this was an attempt to bring collections to potential audiences who could not physically visit, it was unsatisfying. As technology progressed, and, more importantly, as understanding of what was possible through technology grew, institutions began to utilize the new medium in completely new ways to foster understanding of the art and artifacts at their disposal. Now a visitor could zoom in to see the artist's brushstrokes, click on a hyperlink for more information according to individual interest, create and share his or her own curatorial vision of available objects, and write responses that could be posted so others could read. These experiences do not diminish the importance of the "real." But they are valid, useful, important and exciting in and of themselves.

It would seem that the field is in a similar learning curve with attempts to use virtual or blended instruction to teach collections to groups of participants who may be "attending" programs from a great distance. Many webinars, for example, are following the same model a lecture would if the participants were physically present in the room. A speaker presents on his or her chosen topic, and the presentation is augmented by a Power

Point slide show. There are those who would argue against the educational effectiveness of this sort of presentation in general, but when the audience is present in the same space as the speaker, at the very least politeness dictates that they keep their eyes on the presentation and make an effort to focus, so that they laugh, nod or respond at appropriate times. When the experience is virtual, however, it is easy to become distracted at home by the cute antics of the family pet, or by email in the office, or by anything else actually present in the room.

In adopting this new instructional possibility of virtual or blended learning, many institutions offering educational seminars and courses are still clinging to approaches that work in physical space, while tentatively experimenting with the tools of technology that are unique and potentially powerful. We are lucky that William Crow and Herminia Din have been at the forefront of this exploration and have been willing to share the successes and the challenges of finding the best practices of creating educational experiences with these new tools. In their first book, *Unbound by Place or Time: Museums and Online Learning* (The AAM Press, 2009), they explored the creation and delivery of a distance learning experience, making use of a variety of communication and instructional technology tools for collaboration and engagement. They took us through the steps of choosing approaches, folding in participatory learning in an online environment and community-building among participants. With this new book, the authors take us beyond the initial explorations and present us with case studies that illustrate the continuing challenges and the ever changing potentials of online learning spaces.

One of the greatest potentials of these new learning environments is the ability to foster collaboration between institutions and individuals. As a general trend over the last decade, institutions have been finding that it is more beneficial, and a much more positive act, to work together to meet the needs of our communities rather than compete against each other. Collaboration among institutions promotes the sharing of resources and complementary strengths in ways that allow the partners to achieve goals that would not have been possible on their own. Twenty-first-century technologies open the world for potential collaborations. Physical proximity is no longer a prerequisite for finding a collaborative partner or partners for a program where participants need to be able to explore all of the available collections. When it comes to inter-institutional partnerships, the world is quite literally our oyster. For the participants, the potential for real collaboration is also key. Collaborative learning among individuals supports not only achievement of mutual learning goals, but also, when used among professionals, can help build sustained communities that extend after the initial shared experience has been completed. This aspect is especially important to teachers and other education professionals who can experience a sense of isolation in their day-to-day classrooms.

Collaboration is not easy. Integrating and using new technologies in effective ways is not easy. Education is not easy. Just as the best educational practice acknowledges that there is no one-size-fits all solution for learners, and the best educators differentiate to meet different student needs, the best designers of collaborative museum programs will need to differentiate to suit the different missions, collections, and resources of the institutions. Crow and Din provide a guide through the self-examination needed to choose the best approaches for teaching our collections in virtual learning spaces. Questions that need to be explored in order to ensure success range from the simple decision to collaborate in the first place and deciding whom to collaborate with, to the more complex issues of how technology can assist and deepen the collaboration between institutions, between the participants and the educators, and between the individual participants themselves. Just as our classroom-based colleagues have realized that sitting students at a table does not a collaborative experience make, Crow and Din make clear that having a variety of people simply log on at one time does not ensure a collaborative educational experience. With this book, however, the authors have given the field a tool kit for making use of the wonderful resources available to us in the world of interactive and instructional technologies that can bring us all together in such wonderful ways.

Lynda Kennedy, M.S.Ed., Ph.D.,
director, Teaching & Learning, Literacy and Outreach
New York Public Library

PREFACE

By William Crow and Herminia Din

The story of how we met is probably not a likely one, especially for the opening passages of a museum publication. It's not a story of a coincidental meeting due to a last-minute calendar change, or the fortuitous connection that we sometimes see in movies, when two people bump into one another a street corner.

In the fall of 2006, after hearing multiple encouraging statements from museum friends and colleagues along the lines of "You know who you should meet?" and "There's someone you should connect with," we decided to make a phone call to one another. Although today neither one of us can recall all of the details of that first call, or even who initiated it, we recollect that there was certainly a substantial passage in our conversation about Herminia's Alaskan lifestyle, and some chat about Will's recent apartment renovation. But after these initial minutes of getting to know one another and sharing mutual connections, the conversation turned to a key question: "So what are you working on now?"

This phone call in the fall of 2006, our first conversation with one another, slowly evolved into an ongoing, long-distance collaboration over the past five years. We quickly learned about our mutual interest in interactive technologies and museum-based learning, and how the new landscape of online and blended collaboration could potentially change the field. We brainstormed and debated, sometimes by phone, other times through shared documents online and wikis, and eventually began to develop the first of many blended teacher-training programs that would transform our approach to learning in the museum. We each brought our own expertise and passion to these conversations and interactions, seeing our newfound projects as creative challenges. One might describe our intensive work process as a "flow" experience as we immersed ourselves in the projects, often losing track of time and place. Perhaps because we had become so accustomed to working together closely, we were both shocked in March of 2008, 17 months after our initial phone conversation and after collaborating on several projects and programs, that we still had not met face to face. We finally did get to see one another—in New Orleans in April, 2008, at the National Art Education Association Conference.

In 2009 we published our first book, *Unbound by Place or Time: Museums and Online Learning* (The AAM Press). In that first book, we describe the potential of online learning for museums, and outline the basic how-to's and key strategies when developing an online learning program. Only two years later, the digital world that we explore in the book continues to change at a rapid pace. Today we see ourselves even more deeply immersed in an Internet-based culture. Social networking has taken a substantial place in our daily lives, new online tools encourage us to customize or "mash up" media as we wish, and interactive mobile technologies allow us to draw upon the infinite resources of the Internet at any time and at any place, including inside museums.

We see these changes and innovations as terrifically exciting—not as a celebration of the new media and technologies themselves, but for the possibilities that they offer to people. As we shift from the Information Age to the Collaboration Age, these new technologies offer people the ability to work together in ways that simply weren't possible even 15 years ago. And, although museums draw strength from their unique physical collections and locations, they also now see themselves as digital collections and communities, located in an increasingly global world. We are also enthusiastic to see strong alignment between learner-centric, constructivist approaches to learning in the museum, and the ongoing movement in technology toward a user-centric, collaborative online world. This flattening and democratizing of both educational practice and technological trends offer museums the possibility to engage visitors, and their staffs, in ways that maximize the institution's public value.

We hope that this book is useful for all types of museum professionals, and also for those who are interested in online collaboration more broadly. Although we both self-identify as museum educators, and see educators as key stakeholders and potential leaders in the field of online collaborative learning, this book is intended for all museum professionals who have an interest in contributing to these online educational possibilities. Curatorial and conservation staff, digital media, IT, communications and marketing, visitor services, development and fundraising, and we hope, museum administrators and leaders, will see this book as a spark to begin conversations about the possibilities that online collaborative learning can offer the museum, and museum visitors.

Similar to our first book, we have focused our attention on the concepts and strategies involved in online collaboration, rather than giving focus to the technological tools themselves. Because these tools change on an almost daily basis, we have referred to some key resources within the text and endnotes, but encourage the reader to seek out the new and ever-expanding online tools that become available.

Collaborative online teaching and learning offer exciting potential for exchange among museum professionals, content experts, and visitors, and can lead to cross-institutional and cross-disciplinary content development and new ways of maximizing institutions' role in society. Through this new, shared model of meaning-making, and by re-framing our museum collections in a highly connected, global world, online collaborative learning offers museums and visitors new possibilities for learning, both in small, "narrowcast" groups and also at the larger institutional level. As digital artifacts are created and improved by co-experts working together online toward a common goal, the larger public may benefit from a shared content model, or "digital commons," thus shifting museums from their roles as cultural competitors toward a new model of cultural collaborators.

We hope that you share our excitement and enthusiasm for the possibilities, and that you see your own institution as a learning laboratory in which online collaborative learning may support your goals and your museum's mission.

INTRODUCTION: Shared Spaces

On December 24, 1968, during the Apollo 8 mission to the moon, the astronaut William Anders clicked the shutter on his camera to capture one of the most famous images ever taken. The image was of the planet Earth as seen from the bleak landscape of the moon, the upper portion of the sphere illuminated by the sun. The photograph, which came to be known as *Earthrise,* is often cited as one of the key images to rally the environmental movement, since its message is strikingly clear: we live together, in a single, shared space.

We are all constantly reminded that we live, work, and interact with others in shared spaces. In our daily lives we share our homes, offices, shopping malls, public parks, and of course, institutions, such as museums and libraries. People come together to meet face to face, to exchange ideas and information. We work together to complete transactions that need to happen for us to live our lives.

The virtual world has multiplied our capacity for creating and populating shared spaces, and perhaps has also expanded our uses for these types of shared spaces. We can create and access information and ideas digitally across physical boundaries, and across time. Digital spaces have sparked new practices and possibilities for engaging communication and collaboration that we have not experienced in an analog form.[1]

Through ever-expanding and increasingly efficient participatory digital platforms, shared online spaces offer museums the opportunity to build, exchange, create, and collaborate. These shared digital spaces are often a fusion of words, graphics, mediums, and expansive links to resources that satisfy our growing need, and our visitors' growing need, for convenient and instant access to information. This new digital landscape also has a significant impact on how we learn and interact—whether stimulating a greater debate through the use of collaborative tools or opening possibilities for exploration and simulation in a virtual world.

In these increasingly accessible digital spaces, we can communicate and collaborate—as individuals, or as institutions. Here is a recent example of two institutions from two continents coming together to share their digital resources and spaces to build new learning content.

• • • Museums Working Together in a Shared Space: An Example

In the spring of 2010, the American Museum of Natural History (AMNH) and the National Museum of Natural Science (NMNS) in Taiwan began to discuss a possible collaborative project to share and exchange their digital resources and extend their outreach to global audiences. This project was intended to exploit the content of the NMNS' digital archives of Taiwanese butterflies, and AMNH would develop an online feature at its renowned OLogy site.[2] OLogy is a Web site created in 2001 for kids to learn more about astronomy, paleontology, and the definitions of other "ologies," and to collect OLogy cards (currently 339 cards exactly) during their process of discovery.

Building upon the success of the OLogy site, NMNS proposed to use its digital archives and educational resources, following the Creative Commons[3] framework, and work with AMNH to build a new feature focusing on Taiwan butterflies. Its content would be permanently hosted on AMNH's server. This allowed AMNH the freedom to share and remix the content, with mutual respect and an understanding of the expectations of interpretation and the final visual presentation. Mutual promotion of the butterfly-themed websites was set up by AMNH at their OLogy web site, and by NMNS in a Butterfly of Formosa special exhibition. Advertisements and promotions of the OLogy site were also available to Taiwanese children through NMNS e-newsletters and periodicals.

Both teams began their work in the summer of 2010. Over the next three months, the collaboration took place mainly via email, given the reality of the 12-hour time zone difference. The OLogy team utilized the NMNS digital archives to prepare a preliminary text of the feature; NMNS researchers edited the text and provided matching high-resolution images. To gather feedback, the AMNH OLogy team set up an online beta site of the Taiwan Butterfly Feature with a password for researchers and staff at NMNS to revise the text and relevant pictures. "The Taiwan Butterfly Kingdom" feature was launched in December 2010, seven new OLogy cards were created, a PDF document highlighting nine unique butterfly spaces in Taiwan, cross-linked under the "How to Draw a Monarch" section. An external link to NMNS's "Butterfly of Formosa"[4] digital exhibit was embedded.

Fig.1: A New OLogy Feature: The Butterfly Kingdom—A Collaborative Project between AMNH and NMNS

During this year-long process, a true spirit of collaboration emerged. For AMNH, the staff was able to create additional digital content on an existing platform with new information provided by another institution. NMNS was able to increase its international visibility, and make more extensive use of its digital archives and e-learning resources. Most importantly, with such an initiative, the research content was exposed to a broader international audience of users who may not have known either institution before.

In 2009, these two institutions had collaborated to create a temporary exhibit, Darwin,[5] based on AMNH's Darwin[6] exhibit that had opened in late 2005. Traditionally, many museums collaborate to create traveling or temporary exhibits. But this was the first time these two institutions came together to share digital content. No doubt there were challenges along the way. For instance, there was a language struggle with this web feature—to determine how to craft English and Chinese phrases that dealt with the usage of butterfly symbols in the context of aboriginal culture. NMNS's scientists had their own specifications that needed to be respected, as they required that every butterfly image on the site be a species identified on Taiwan Island only. Clearly the time difference between New York City and Taipei was another challenge, and many correspondences and communications did not happen spontaneously. At times, both parties in the collaboration added their own ideas to further develop and expand the site. The OLogy team added a map of Taiwan on the site, a heart-warming surprise to the NMNS staff. Trust was developed in the process. They also recognized that bringing the work of international scientists into OLogy is valuable for children in the U.S., as well as those in Taiwan and around the globe. One of the primary goals of OLogy is to introduce children to many of the people who do science around the world, and the different kinds of work that they do.

This project also demonstrates that institutional collaboration can add significant value to a project, but as with any high quality media project, it is production-intensive. The time and effort of each team must be carefully measured and accounted for. As Karen Taber, Senior Project Manager on behalf of the OLogy team, stated in a recent email: "This project has given us more information about what is involved in a collaboration so that we can more effectively cost out the total need that would be required to support future opportunities."[7]

Finally, the rewards were greater for each institution, and the outcomes of the collaboration benefited the public on a global scale. As the participants learned from this project, as long as we are willing to share space, time, and trust in a digital, global age, increased collaboration is an attainable goal.

••• All Together Now

Living and working in a new, digitally connected world, it is becoming increasingly clear that our actions and our achievements in these new shared spaces are what matter most. We can collectively create and innovate in ways that simply weren't possible even 15 years ago. This new environment for living and learning is an exciting one for museum professionals, as we strive to find new ways of increasing our institutions' public value through online access.

As our digital, participatory culture grows and deepens, and as museums begin to embrace online technologies to interact with visitors, these are some of the questions we face: How can people and institutions collaborate in new ways that lead to dynamic and innovative educational experiences with museum visitors, and with one another? How can museums harness these interactive technologies to re-frame their collections, educational programs, and museum practice? In this book, we explore how new methods of online collaboration offer exciting potential for exchange among museum professionals, content experts, and visitors. They can also lead to cross-institutional and cross-disciplinary content development, and new ways of maximizing institutions' public value.

••• Case Study

In the following case study, Michael Edson, Director of Web and New Media Strategy for the Smithsonian Institution, discusses a recent initiative, Smithsonian Commons. This collaborative project involves 19 museums and galleries, nine research centers, 168 affiliate museums, 137 million objects, artworks, and specimens in its collection, and 6.4 million digitized objects available online. By creating a shared digital space, a "commons," the Smithsonian can now provide the public—locally and globally—with access to the collections and expertise in new ways.

Endnotes

1 Through new websites like Groupon.com we work collaboratively with our neighbors to access bargains from local businesses. We can use our mobile technologies with sites such as FourSquare.com to "check in" at locations, see who else is engaged in the same activity, and even become the virtual mayor as we take ownership of shared spaces.

2 Go to OLogy site for more details. http://www.amnh.org/ology/

3 See www.creativecommons.org, a nonprofit organization that develops, supports, and stewards legal and technical infrastructure that maximizes digital creativity, sharing, and innovation.

4 Butterfly of Formosa Digital Exhibit, http://digimuse.nmns.edu.tw/formosabutterfly/en/index.html

5 NMNS Darwin Exhibit, http://www.nmns.edu.tw/nmns_eng/04exhibit/Temporary/exhibitis/DARWIN.htm

6 AMNH Darwin exhibit, http://www.amnh.org/exhibitions/darwin/

7 Karen Taber, Senior Project Manager, National Center for Science Literacy, Education, & Technology American Museum of Natural History, e-mail message to author, January 19, 2011.

THE COMMONS:
Helping People Get Stuff Done

By Michael Edson

There's a certain energy to somebody who is making something, learning something, or solving a problem. There's an intensity of focus, a sense of urgency, a twinkle in the eye. We know on a deeply personal level and as a society that *doing things matters*—whether the thing being done is for practical or scholarly purposes, economic gain, altruism, for formal education or self-directed learning, or just for the pure joy of it. We accord special status to those whom President Barack Obama called "The risk-takers, the doers, the makers of things..."[1] These "makers" are important—the future of our species might quite literally depend on their success, and with great pride we fill our museums with evidence of the things they've figured out and accomplished.[2] Museums are celebrations of human doing—but here we have a disconnect: while museums excel at celebrating things that makers have thought and done in the past, they can be surprisingly indifferent to the needs of people who want to get stuff done *in the present and in the future.*

There are nearly 18,000 museums in the USA and together they spend more than $20.7 billion every year to accomplish their work in society.[3] That's a lot of cash! That's more than the annual gross domestic products of almost half the nations on earth.[4] Museums have many of the raw ingredients that creators, innovators, problem solvers—*makers*—need. Museums have vast collections of rare and notable physical and intellectual property, they have people with expertise and know-how. They nurture curiosity and knowledge creation through research, publication, exhibition, and public programming. They hold positions of trust and respect in their communities and they're heralded as places that "reflect creativity, history, culture, ideas, innovation, exploration, discovery, diversity, freedom of expression and the ideals of democracy."[5] Wow! With all this, museums are in a great position to help people innovate and do new things!

But walk into any museum in the country and ask these three questions:

1. Can I get access to all your collections and resources?
   These are raw materials for creation and innovation

2. Are experts available to help me understand key ideas and concepts?
   Experts are guides, connectors, and problem-solvers—whether they work for museums directly or are part of their broader networks

3. Can I incorporate your collections and resources into new products, ideas, or creative works?
   Once I get raw materials and expertise, can I do new things with them?

My sense is that the public expects the answers to these questions to be yes,[6] many museum employees want the answers to be yes, and makers need the answers to be yes, but with some notable exceptions the answer to these questions is likely to be either a highly conditional yes or an outright no.

And many in the public have noticed.

The comments below are from over 1,200 public responses to the Smithsonian Commons Prototype, a website set up in 2010 to explore the implications of opening up access to Smithsonian resources, expertise, and communities.[7]

One of my biggest gripes doing presentations for the public on archaeology, is the number of museums that do not have their collections online. Much is kept hidden away for researchers only. We can read journal articles on valuable exhibits and sometimes a few drawings are available, but anything else requires either a visit or an application to do scholarly research. This is not fair to the public, since they pay either directly or indirectly for the valuable items kept for a limited number of people. Further, many people cannot travel or will never travel to see some more distant institutions. I am hoping for the day when all museums small and large put their collections online, for the benefit of schools, colleges and the general public. (Excerpt from comment #406)

I would like to see larger images of artifacts... I'd like to see images of the over 90% of your collection that is neither digitally available now, or sitting in your archives. (Excerpt from comment #548)

Images, expert lecturers, animations, related stories/references--all these would be nice to have easy access to, instead of searching through the whole internet and trying to mine gems that way. (Excerpt from comment #87)

I love the fact that [in the Smithsonian Commons Prototype] you can cut and paste pictures for reports!!!! Copyright is such a headache for students. (Comment #163)

...one of the great qualities of the Web is the ability to share and access information around the world, and I commend the Smithsonian for its effort in getting its wealth of resources outside all of its walls. (Excerpt from comment #989)

Yes, please to APIs. A commons is fabulous, but much more fabulous when it exists outside a silo, and can be blended with other free and licensed resources available through a library. (Comment #22)

I want to explore all the resources the Smithsonian has. I'm a high school student interested in every science from astronomy to physical/forensic anthropology to biology to robotics. (Comment #222)

[I'd like to] download high-resolution images and photographs that I can use in my work. (Comment #50)

Most museums aren't focused on people like this. People like this, with practical digital requirements, didn't exist 20 years ago! Most museum management philosophies have been forged by the traditional responsibilities of caring for physical collections, academic research, and bricks-and-mortar visitation.[8] Physical collections are unique and fragile; subject matter experts and other museum staff are busy and need to be protected from the unrelenting demands of the public; researchers are given access based on their scholarly credentials; intellectual property needs to be restricted to protect the interests of rights holders, to prevent erroneous interpretation, and to generate revenue.

And while we in the museum world are dealing with these issues the culture is moving on without us.

Tentative investments and weak governance for new media in museums, and difficulties recognizing emergent paradigms for collaboration, innovation, and knowledge sharing, have created an environment where museums' relevance, brand identity, and impact have been successfully challenged by unexpected online rivals.[9]

And if the Internet has shown museums one thing, it is that if people can't get what they need from us, they'll go elsewhere.[10]

New Models

We know from the last decade of watching emerging technologies wreak havoc on the 20th century's venerable institutions that technology opens up disruptive new ways of finding and re-using information and expertise.

- Chris Anderson's *The Long Tail* (Hyperion 2006 and also online at http://www.wired.com/wired/archive/12.10/tail.html) explains how productive online audiences form around niche content.
- David Weinberger's *Everything is Miscellaneous* (Times Books, 2007) explains the ways in which making information digital changes the way it can be organized, found and used.
- Don Tapscott and Anthony Williams' *Wikinomics* (Penguin, 2006) describes new forms of collaboration and commercial enterprise and Clay Shirky's *Here Comes Everybody* (Hyperion, 2008) describes new forms of collective action.
- Lawrence Lessig's *The Future of Ideas* (Random House, 2001) and James Boyle's *The Public Domain* (Yale University Press, 2008) describe the powerful relationship between innovation and the intellectual property commons in the digital age.
- Tim O'Reilly's *What is Web 2.0* describes a profoundly important set of new relationships between companies, data, and communities.[11]
- Joy's Law, that "no matter who you are, most of the smartest people work for someone else," summarizes the opportunities of networking and distributed knowledge creation and is a warning against organizational hubris.[12]

- John P. Kotter's *A Sense of Urgency* (Harvard Business Press, 2008) details the rapid acceleration of change in culture and business (mostly caused by information technology) and the dire consequences of inaction.[13]

As these new modes of discovery, collaboration, and knowledge creation gain power, the Smithsonian Institution, like many organizations, is working hard to keep pace. In 2009 the Smithsonian developed its first ever Web and New Media Strategy to communicate the nature of these changes to staff, management, and stakeholders, and to tell a story about how new media can be a catalyst to innovation inside and outside the Institution.[14] The broad vision, inspired by the real accomplishments of web and new media practitioners, represents a shift from thinking about museums primarily as physical venues for personal enrichment towards thinking about museums as significant contributors to broader efforts to achieve societal goals. To these ends, the centerpiece of the Smithsonian's Web and New Media Strategy is the idea of a commons—a new part of our digital presence designed to stimulate creativity, learning, and innovation through open access to Smithsonian resources, communities, and expertise.[15] The commons concept imagines the Smithsonian as a helpful agent and partner to makers, doers, and learners. But what exactly is a commons and how do you build one?

What is a Commons?

Abstractly, a commons is a set of resources maintained in the public sphere for the use and benefit of *everyone*.

Usually, a commons is created when a property owner decides that a given set of resources—grass for grazing sheep, forests for parkland, software code, or intellectual property—will be more valuable if freely shared than if restricted.

In the law, and in our understanding of the way the world works, we recognize that no idea stands alone, and that all innovation is built on the ideas and innovations of others. When creators, scientists, inventors, educators, artists, researchers, business people, entrepreneurs—when *everyone* has access to the raw materials of knowledge, innovation flourishes.

Conversely, unnecessarily restricted content is a barrier to innovation. This is the anti-commons, a thicket of difficulties. If you can't find an idea, can't understand its context, can't leverage your social network (however you define it—perhaps it's just your immediate friends and colleagues) to share and add value to it, and if you can't get legal permission to use, re-use, or make it into something new, then knowledge and innovation suffer. Unnecessarily restricted content is like a virus that spreads through the internet, making the intellectual property provenance of each generation of new ideas less and less clear.

I like to think of a commons as a kind of organized workshop where the raw materials of knowledge and innovation can be found and assembled into new things.[16] This kind of workshop—a place where ideas and knowledge can flow freely and be put to use by industrious and creative people—is harmonious with the needs of makers and the stated missions of many museums, including the Smithsonian.[17]

THE INGREDIENTS OF A COMMONS

There is no design manual for how to create a commons, but from interviews with people involved in commons projects, the maker movement, and my own observations and study, I've come to recognize 13 design attributes that, in combination, lead to positive outcomes for makers of all kinds. For the remainder of this article, think of a commons as a kind of fortifying soup that's made with various combinations of these 13 ingredients.

1. Federated

A commons brings things together that would otherwise be separate. The Smithsonian Collections Search Center helps researchers by bringing together over seven million object records from more than 23 Smithsonian collection information systems. http://collections.si.edu/search/about.jsp

2. Findable

It doesn't do much good to have a bunch of stuff in a commons if you can't find anything. The crowdsourced stock photo site iStockPhoto does a better job helping me find stuff than any museum, library, or archive site I know. Industrial supplier McMaster Carr is a standout as well. http://istockphoto.com and http://mcmastercarr.com

3. Shareable

The whole purpose of putting resources into a commons is so they can be shared and used. A commons is shareable by default. On the Brooklyn Museum Web site, sharing is built right into the platform. http://www.brooklynmuseum.org/opencollection/objects/157722/Morris_Kantor

4. Reusable

Intellectual property policies in a commons are uniform and clearly stated so users know, in advance—without having to ask or beg—that they can incorporate resources from the commons into new works. On Flickr, the copyright and permissions are stated clearly, everywhere. http://flickr.com

5. Free

"Free resources are crucial to innovation and creativity" says Creative Commons founder Lawrence Lessig.[18] Free, Findable, and Shareable form a particularly powerful combination. The Internet Archive says on their home page that "like a paper library, we provide free access..." http://www.archive.org

6. Bulk Download

Sometimes makers need a lot of something, or all of something, to solve a problem. On the Powerhouse Museum's Web site, you can download their entire collection database with one click. http://www.powerhousemuseum.com/collection/database/download.php

7. Machine Readable

Sometimes a maker needs to be able to write a program to work with data—particularly when you've got a lot of it. [19] The information in a commons needs to be understandable to computer programs—machine readable. Data.gov is designed to encourage digital mashups through machine readable formats. http://www.data.gov

8. High Resolution

A commons should make available, for free, the highest quality, highest resolution resources possible. On NASA's Web site, you can download photographs so big that you can see how individual grains of Martian soil were compressed by the wheels of the Mars Rover. The paltry images on most museum Web sites thwart the efforts of researchers and enthusiasts, and undermine our attempts to let the drama and meaning of our collections shine through. http://marsrover.nasa.gov/gallery/panoramas/spirit/

9. Collaboration without Control

Because resources are free, high quality, and sharing and reuse are encouraged, new kinds of collaborative work can take place—are taking place—without needing to involve lawyers, contracts, and bureaucrats.

Clay Shirky, in Here Comes Everybody, writes "we are living in the middle of a remarkable increase in our ability to share, to cooperate with one another, and to take collective action, all outside the framework of traditional institutions and organization... Getting the free and ready participation of a large, distributed group with a variety of skills has gone from impossible to simple."[20]

MIT Open Courseware has case studies of collaborations and partnerships that have come to fruition exactly because MIT did not attempt to assert control over the intellectual property in the Open Courseware collection. http://ocw.mit.edu and http://ocw.mit.edu/about/ocw-stories/triatno-yudo-harjoko/

10. Network Effects

In a commons designed with network effects in mind you get a virtuous cycle: the more the commons is used, the better it becomes, and the better it becomes, the more people will find and use it. Over 180,000 people have added map data to the OpenStreetMap project[21], and those contributions have created a powerful resource that can be used and re-used by anyone, for free. http://www.openstreetmap.org/

11. The Public Domain

The public domain is important. Intellectual property in the public domain is not owned by anybody: it can be used by anyone for any purpose. James Boyle writes that the Public Domain is not "some gummy residue left behind when all the good stuff has been covered by property law. The public domain is the place where we quarry the building blocks of our culture."[22]

12. Designed to Help Real People

Software developer and social media thought leader Kathy Sierra says that every user is a hero in their own epic journey.[23] The job of the Smithsonian Commons is not to broadcast our accomplishments to a passive audience: it's to help real people succeed in their epic quests through life. (See the Smithsonian Web and New Media Strategy at http://smithsonian-webstrategy.wikispaces.com/The+Smithsonian+Commons+--+A+Place+to+Begin)

13. Trust

After thinking about the previous 12 items for a couple of months I've decided that there's a 13th, and that's trust.

Wired magazine founding editor Kevin Kelly said "the network economy is founded on technology, but can only be built on relationships. It starts with chips and ends with trust."[24]

The Smithsonian is in the forever business. By putting something in the Smithsonian Commons—be it a cultural treasure, or a folk song, a fossil of a bug, a lecture, or a community—we'll be asking people to trust us. We're not going to scam you. We're not going to violate your privacy. We're going to be honest about what we do and don't know, we're going to be open to new ideas and points of view, we're going to help each other figure out the world, and these promises are good forever. Museums are among the few organizations in our culture that enter into those kinds of promises, and we take that responsibility very seriously.

LOOKING FORWARD

We are just starting the process of building the Smithsonian Commons. It's a complex endeavor and there will surely be a lot of unknowns and surprises down the road, but I am confident that the defining characteristics of the Smithsonian Commons vision will endure: the desire to help people get things done, on their own terms, with the freedom to use the Smithsonian's resources, communities, and expertise in any way that works.

This is a moment in history when ideas, discovery, and action really matter, and many museum professionals feel that museums, libraries, archives, research organizations—*all* of our beloved public institutions need to muster their resources to help accomplish meaningful work in society. We need to make a difference in the world. The Smithsonian Institution's strategic plan states that we need "to use our vast resources for the public good in the midst of unceasing demographic, technological, and social change..."[25]

Or, as Internet pioneer Howard Rheingold put it in his commentary about the Smithsonian Commons concept,[26]

> *The Smithsonian is not just about the past, but about the present and the future. The Smithsonian is not just about what goes on inside the walls in Washington, D.C., but about the communications that flow through those walls to and from citizens. The Smithsonian is not just about experts teaching citizens, but also about citizens teaching — and discovering knowledge together with — each other.*

Endnotes

1   "Transcript of Barack Obama's Inaugural Address", *New York Times*, January 20, 2009, http://www.nytimes.com/2009/01/20/us/politics/20text-obama.html 12/17/2010.

2   The term "makers" is associated with a movement that celebrates Do It Yourself ("DIY") culture and is traceable to the open source software movement. See Remarks on Innovation, Education, and the Maker Movement by Thomas Kalil of the White House Office of Science and Technology Policy, *O'Reilly Radar* blog, September 29, 2010, http://radar.oreilly.com/2010/10/innovation-education-and-the-m.html.

3   *Museum Financial Information*, 2009, AAM Press, 2009. The exact number of museums cited by AAM's study is 17,744. AAM notes that this number is extrapolated from other data and is not an exact count. The $20.7 billion figure is cited on p. 49.

4   *See International Monetary Fund, World Economic Outlook Database, October 2010: Nominal GDP list of countries, data for the year 2009*, http://www.imf.org/external/pubs/ft/weo/2010/02/weodata/index.aspx. Of the 181 countries whose GDP's are listed by this report, 86 have GDP's under $20.7 billion. Getting the data from this resource directly is a little complex but the Wikipedia has a useful summary at http://en.wikipedia.org/wiki/List_of_countries_by_GDP_(nominal).

5   Slade, Roy, "Why Museums Matter?" (Keynote address presented at the Florida Association of Museums Annual Meeting, Clearwater, FL, September 19, 2010, http://royslade.com/WhyMusemsMatter.aspx. Roy Slade is the Director Emeritus of the Cranbrook Art Museum.

6   When I use the term "the public" I am not using it in the sense of the great unwashed masses. The public is *everyone*, including both Nobel laureates and 8 year-olds.

7   "The Smithsonian Commons Prototype," accessed December 23, 2010, http://www.si.edu/commons/prototype. Public comments are listed at http://smithsonian-webstrategy.wikispaces.com/Public+Comments+on+Smithsonian+Commons+Prototype+0001-0200 . Also see the video of interviews with Smithsonian visitors:

"Mashup for Smithsonian Web and New Media Strategy." http://www.youtube.com/watch?v=MTJ8u2HGtrs.

8   American Association of Museum accreditation standards are largely driven by these factors. The accreditation process I participated in during 2006-2007 included only one cursory question regarding web and new media activities. See Accreditation Standards, http://www.aam-us.org/museumresources/accred/standards.cfm.

9   AAM Museum Financial Information, 2009 says that median Internet and website expenses for American museums is $5,113 per year, just 0.4 percent of total operating expenses, though they note that further research is needed to understand if the number reported is truly representative of all expenses (p. 106). Overall, my assertions about investment and governance are based on my own observations after more than 85 web strategy presentations and workshops during 2009 and 2010. Some of my conclusions can be found in my presentations "Ten Patterns for Organizational Change" (http://www.slideshare.net/edsonm/michael-edson-ten-patterns-for-organizational-change) and "The Digital Strategy Thermocline" (http://www.slideshare.net/edsonm/michael-edson-brown-university-digital-strategy-thermocline)

Challenges to traditional notions of trust, reputation, and relevance in museums are explored in greater detail in Edson, M., Fast, Open, and Transparent: Developing the Smithsonian's Web and New Media Strategy. In J. Trant and D. Bearman (eds). Museums and the Web 2010: Proceedings. Toronto: Archives & Museum Informatics. Published March 31, 2010, http://www.archimuse.com/mw2010/papers/edson/edson.html.

10   I have found ample evidence of this at the Smithsonian and other institutions: cursory Internet searches for "our" content often lead to places where the public have re-used and expanded upon our content, or made substitutions for materials they could have gotten from us but apparently could not find or could not get permission to use. Some examples are documented in "Imagining the Smithsonian Commons" (http://www.slideshare.net/edsonm/cil-2009-michael-edson-text-version) and "Prototyping the Smithsonian Commons" (http://www.slideshare.net/edsonm/michael-edson-prototyping-the-smithsonian-commons)

To further extend the point, Nick Poole, CEO of the Collections Trust, UK, said in his keynote at the 2010 New Zealand Digital Forum "So this new consumer, the people who we have to be ready to serve as museums, libraries, and archives, is social with their technology--they're playful, they're collaborative. They're purposeful, they're resourceful. If you place an obstruction in their way they'll find a way around it. if you present content that can't be re-used then they'll either use it anyway or they'll find a way of discovering the content elsewhere in a way that can be...That shift in the basic expectations of consumers has happened already." Nick's keynote can be downloaded from http://www.r2.co.nz/20101018/, and the portion quoted above begins at 16:25.

11   O'Reilly, Tim, "Web 2.0: Design Patterns and Business Models for the Next Generation of Software," September 30, 2005, http://www.oreillynet.com/pub/a/oreilly/tim/news/2005/09/30/what-is-web-20.html.

12   Joy's Law is frequently referenced in business and strategy contexts without academic source attribution. A suitable primary reference seems to be Lakhani KR, Panetta JA, "The Principles of Distributed Innovation," 2007, http://papers.ssrn.com/sol3/papers.cfm?abstract_id=1021034.

13 A podcast interview with Kotter, "The Importance of Urgency," provides an engaging overview of the book, http://www.bnet.com/blog/intercom/the-importance-of-urgency-hbr-ideacast/1869.

14 Note that "Fast, Open, and Transparent: Developing the Smithsonian's Web and New Media Strategy" (2009) provides background and details about the Smithsonian's web and New Media Strategy process.

The Smithsonian's Web and New Media Strategy is available for download at http://www.si.edu/About/Policies. The Strategy is also available on the wiki on which it was created: http://smithsonian-webstrategy.wikispaces.com/Strategy+--+Table+of+Contents.

15 From the Smithsonian Web and New Media Strategy, Section IV. The Smithsonian Commons, a Place to Begin, http://smithsonian-webstrategy.wikispaces.com/The+Smithsonian+Commons+--+A+Place+to+Begin.

16 Note that in a physical commons there is competition for physical resources. Only so many sheep can graze in a single pasture before it's all used up. This is where the phrase "the tragedy of the commons" comes from, but lawyers say that digital resources in a commons are "non-rivalrous"—there's no rivalry for them. We can all download all the pictures in a digital commons over and over again and they never run out. All of our sheep can eat the same digital grass to their heart's content.

17 The Smithsonian Institution's mission is "the increase and diffusion of knowledge." See http://www.si.edu/About/Mission.

18 Lessig, Lawrence. *The Future of Ideas: The Fate of the Commons in a Connected World*. New York: Random House, 2001, p. 14

19 I borrowed this pattern from "Eight Principles of Open Government Data," December, 2007. http://resource.org/8_principles.html.

20 Shirky, Clay, Here Comes Everybody, New York, Hyperion, 2008, p 21.

21 "Online Maps: Everyman Offers New Directions," New York Times, November 11, 2009.

22 Boyle, James, *The Public Domain: Enclosing the Commons of the Mind,* New Haven and London, Yale University Press, 2008, p. 40. The Computer & Communications Industry Association estimates that public domain, fair use, and other forms of non-copyright content contributed $4.7 trillion to the U.S. economy in 2007, and industries that benefit from this type of intellectual property employ 1 in six workers in the U.S. (See "Fair Use in the U.S. Economy. Computer and Communications Industry Association," April 27, 2010, http://www.ccianet.org/index.asp?sid=5&artid=158.)

An example of public domain content is the endless stream of meteorological data that NOAA pumps into the public domain. Weather.com, the Weather Channel, and almost every weather forecast you've ever seen can trace its ancestry back to public domain data from this government agency.

23 From Twitter, @kathysierra, November 5, 2009: "I'm your user. I'm supposed to be the protagonist. I'm on a hero's hourney. Your company should be the mentor/helpful sidekick. Not an orc." Sierra's Web site is *Creating Passionate Users,* http://headrush.typepad.com/.

24 Green, David L. Ed. iQuote: *Brilliance and Banter from the Internet Age*, Connecticut, Lyons Press, 2008, p. 50

25 "Smithsonian Institution: Inspiring Generations Through Knowledge and Discovery, Fiscal Years 2010–2015," (published in February, 2010), http://www.si.edu/About/Policies, p. 5.

26 From the Smithsonian Commons Prototype, 2010. This is an excerpt from Howard Rheingold's comments about the Smithsonian Commons concept at http://www.si.edu/commons/prototype/comments.html. Rheingold's comment continues: "The Smithsonian Commons is not just about using contemporary technology to further an enterprise that was founded with deep respect for American technological innovation, but about expanding the idea of the institution itself. Every click on a website, every video viewed, every exhibition shared via mobile device, every citizen scientist project, every teacher and student interaction with the Smithsonian via social media expands the idea of what the Smithsonian Institution is, who it reaches, what it can do."

The URL above points to many other comments about the Smithsonian Commons concept from thought-leaders, bloggers, and others.

PART ONE: Online Collaborative Learning

We think, work, and live in shared spaces. Today, given the multitude of dynamic and pervasive digital technologies, we interact in ways and in environments that simply weren't possible until recently. But of course it isn't enough that we simply co-exist in a shared space—physically or virtually. What matters is what occurs in that space. How can we work together, collaboratively, toward some shared purpose or goal? How do these new technologies help us collaborate?

WHAT IS ONLINE COLLABORATIVE LEARNING?

Online collaborative learning is the process through which teachers and learners—collaborators—work together through a networked environment (the Internet) toward a shared purpose or goal. Online collaborative learning may help support collaborators who also meet face to face, or these collaborators may not meet together in person at all. Online collaborative learning can occur under the auspices of a formal course, program, or project, or people may connect with one another informally online to satisfy their own interests, curiosities, or co-create a digital project. Online collaborative learning can occur over long periods of time (weeks, months, even years), or for short, sporadic periods, depending on the nature and purpose of the endeavor. But in successful online collaborative learning, the participants are invested, are connected, and have opportunities to transform the outcome.

Online learning is a topic that is becoming increasingly familiar to many. While online learning was once considered to be exclusively the domain of higher education, it continues to expand to K-12 education, alternative education settings, cultural institutions, and even into our daily lives as we communicate via e-mail, social networks, and instant messaging. While we might not initially consider our daily electronic communication to have an educational value or purpose, these experiences often contain learning opportunities. Social media connects us with the daily lives of friends and family. We witness their travels, their interactions and responses. As we check the latest news online on sites such as nytimes.com, we not only receive the bold print headlines, but can share our own ideas, and comment on the posts by others. The proliferation of blogs brings us in contact with voices and ideas that were unimagined 15 years ago. Granted, the latest gossip about Hollywood celebrities may not be what you had in mind in terms of educational value. But in the end, even blog gurus like Perez Hilton and his followers have the potential to teach us something.

The collaborative aspect of online learning is an essential ingredient, and will receive much of our attention throughout this book. In earlier phases, critics of online learning claimed that online interactions had a "call and response" format. An instructor posts a question and others dutifully respond in lockstep. While this certainly still occurs in some realms of online learning, this does not have to be the paradigm. Recently online learning has evolved toward a more collaborative endeavor due to a number of factors.

First, in the past several decades, educators increasingly see the value of learner-centric, participatory approaches in order to involve learners and deepen understanding, but also to improve the outcomes. Building on the tenets of constructivist thinking and progressive education, this direction is increasingly at the core of the educational practice in museums and other settings. Second, new digital technologies allow us to work together and collaborate in new ways. While in the past it may have been possible only to post responses to a threaded discussion, or to add a comment, today participants are increasingly able to be co-creators, co-authors, co-producers. These online collaborators have the power to change content online using wiki-based technologies or shared documents; they can add their voices in new and more dynamic ways through multimedia, such as audio or video; they can build upon, re-purpose, and share existing digital information. Through these new forms of interaction, we see the possibilities for greater innovation, increased creativity, better productivity—and potentially, more expansive and dynamic learning.

HOW IS ONLINE COLLABORATIVE LEARNING DIFFERENT
FROM TRADITIONAL FACE-TO-FACE INTERACTION?
HOW DOES WORKING TOGETHER ONLINE EMPOWER
COLLABORATORS IN NEW WAYS?

In many ways, learning together online isn't so different from face-to-face learning. All participants come together around a central topic, problem, or goal, and work together. Each contributes, drawing upon his or her strengths, and over time, progress is made toward the end result. Similar to contemporary learning practices, the role of each participant can vary, including the role of the teacher. As teachers and learners become more involved and increase participation and input, the goal, process, and product may shift and change.

But working collaboratively online toward an educational purpose has some key differences from face-to-face learning. For one, and most obviously, the participants aren't necessarily working face-to-face or even in real time. While this mode of working and learning can be a challenge, or even a bit unsettling for first-time online collaborators, it can have advantages. Perhaps the greatest advantage is that the collaborators can be brought together across place and time—including people who would never have been able to participate in a face-to-face setting. This means that anyone who can get connected via a computer and the Internet is a potential collaborator. It is hard to overemphasize exactly how important and exciting this change is. Experts in the field, participants from diverse countries and continents, and even and especially participants who hold views and experiences quite different from our own, can potentially collaborate.[1]

Online collaboration also differs from face-to-face collaboration because the means, or tools with which we are working and communicating, have a strong impact on not only how we work, but also what we can produce. We can instantly exchange ideas through a networked environment, and we can immediately bring in the endless resources and information that the Internet offers to deepen and expand our conversations—all of this captured and documented online. Online collaborators may even express themselves differently from face-to-face encounters. Rather than relying on text or words, online collaborators might use video, photos, music, a link to a website or other multimedia to express an idea or provide information. A third way that online collaborative learning differs from face-to-face learning models is that through online collaboration we are not only working together with our own group of collaborators, but we have the ability, if we choose, to share that work, and our working process, with others in a way that is accessible to a broader public and can continue over time. While sometimes we may collaborate online within a "closed" private group (such as a Ning site or Google group), at other times we can work together in semi-public or fully public ways that bring in other stakeholders, perhaps for the duration of the project, or just for one short visit.

Online collaborative learning can be a powerful way for participants to interact, share, and create. But beyond the initial novelty of seeing or communicating with people online, or the fun of co-editing and co-creating documents or files, there is a key aspect that we should emphasize: collaborating online can lead to innovation. It has the possibility to create new types of communities of learners and co-creators, and can stimulate our own critical, creative, and reflective thinking.[2]

WHAT FORMS CAN ONLINE COLLABORATIVE LEARNING TAKE?

Online collaborative learning can take many different forms, depending on the purpose. The technology tools themselves can often be flexible and adaptable, and a single platform or tool can often be used in many different ways. While we might first think of online collaborative learning as taking the form of a class or a specific project, it can occur in many different guises, and through various types of media and platforms. Here are a few ways that online collaborative learning can occur:

> **Online-Only.** People working together online who never meet face-to-face. They might have opportunities for live interaction using synchronous technologies (such as Skype or a webcam), but may not see one another at all. They might also be online at different times (working asynchronously) and contribute different parts or components. Some examples of online-only programs or projects can could be virtual world events in Second Life, or a live webinar.

Online-Enhanced. These types of programs or projects utilize online collaborative technologies to supplement or enhance a primarily in-person experience. An example of this might be a face-to-face university course in which the online technology is used as holding place for sharing document or other resources.

Blended Learning. The in-person and the online components of the educational experience are seen as complementary to one another, and both of these components build off one another. A recent U.S. Department of Education study found that blended learning educational models hold much promise in terms of their impact.[3]

Websites That Invite User-Generated Content. Years ago when websites were first developed, they were seen as places simply to broadcast information to passive, browsing viewers. Today websites are places where visitors are often contributors, and where the interaction is not only between the creator of the website and the visitors but also between and among the visitors. For example, TripAdvisor.com is a place that is essentially driven by the users themselves, and the site visitors learn from one another through sharing experiences.

Social Media for Collaboration. While we may be most familiar with social networks for their social function, these platforms can also be harnessed for their educational value. The K-12 educational world has used social network sites such as Ning.com extensively for teacher groups and professional development projects.

BUT HOW CAN ONLINE COLLABORATIVE LEARNING HAVE VALUE FOR MUSEUMS AND THEIR VISITORS? WHAT ARE THE BENEFITS?

Museums are uniquely poised to take advantage of online collaborative learning. First, museums are places that have rich content. Their physical collections, digital assets, and staff are all resources that the public, locally and globally, would like to access. Second, museums have been progressively moving toward more visitor-centric models for the past 100 years, and the new possibilities that technology offers is a new means for museums to build on this trend.[4] Free-choice learning, in which visitors can create their own experiences and meaning, is a central part of museum-based learning, which parallels the type of thinking and creation that can happen in an online collaborative environment. Third, museums can be social spaces for learning, and online collaborative learning invites, and even requires, that participants interact with one another and contribute their own unique assets and skills. And finally, by using online collaborative learning, museums have new ways of learning more about their visitors, resulting in a new type of research, and even professional development, for the institution.

SOME THEORETICAL FRAMEWORKS THAT SUPPORT ONLINE COLLABORATIVE LEARNING

In addition to some of the practical and innovative aspects that online collaborative learning can offer, there are a number of theoretical frameworks from the fields of education, media, and cognitive science that can illuminate and support these ideas. Here is a brief summary of key ideas that one might consider from each of these fields:

Constructivism and Progressive Education

In the early 20th century, the American philosopher and educator John Dewey wrote extensively about the need for educative experiences—those that connect to the lives and relevancies of the learners. Dewey believed that learners needed to be immersed in real-world tasks, experiences, and communities, and that school reform needed to incorporate these elements. In his work *Democracy and Education*, Dewey also speaks about what defines a learning community, and how physical proximity may not necessarily be needed:

> Persons do not become a society by living in physical proximity, any more than a man ceases to be socially influenced by being so many feet or miles removed from others. A book or a letter may institute a more intimate association between human beings separated thousands of miles from each other than exists between dwellers under the same roof.[5]

Jean Piaget and Lev Vygotsky, developmental and educational psychologists, pioneered the fields of social and environmental factors that impacted learners. Piaget developed the sociological model of development in the 1920s, positing that children move from an ego-centric view of the world to more sociocentric models. Vygotsky is perhaps best known for his theories relating to the zone of proximal development, in which learners must be challenged by others and by situations to an extent that is effective for the learner.[6]

Media Theory

In the realm of media theory, Marshall McLuhan predicted in the 1960s that we would soon be living in a "global village," connected by networks of communications that would bring cultures and communities into close contact. He also declared that the media itself had great impact on the messages that are crafted, and even that the medium itself should be carefully examined for the messages that are embodied within it. McLuhan theorized about the amounts of participation that different forms of media required. These theories of "hot" and "cold" media posited that people are invited to respond and participate in different ways, depending on the medium at hand, and that our perceptions of the messages embedded within it can vary.[7]

More recently, the media analyst Henry Jenkins, formerly of the MIT Media Lab, has described our time in a moment of technological and cultural convergence. Through massive and rapid changes in technologies, and in the ways that participants are interacting with one another, we are moving into a world where our collective stories and ideas are shaped in fluid, dynamic ways, and across multiple platforms.[8] Other researchers and authors such as Clay Shirky and Thomas Friedman have posited that we are living in a flattened world of heightened engagement by many diverse stakeholders, which necessarily changes the way that we produce, create, and engage with one another.[9]

Cognitive Theory and Computer Science

The new and expansive field of cognitive science, which has emerged in the last 75 years, is often described as being at the intersection of many fields of study: psychology, linguistics, anthropology, economics, education, measurement and evaluation. Cognitive science also has roots in computer science, as researchers saw computers as "thinking machines," and saw relationships between the operations of the mind and the construction of artificial intelligence.

During World War II, military researchers studying problems of perception, attention, judgment, and decision-making came in contact with other professionals, such as communications specialists and engineers. By studying such topics as pilot error or the performance of soldiers, these wartime researchers began to broaden the field of psychology to include theories not only about human memory and cognition, but also about how those thinking processes are influenced by different tools and situations.[10]

The 1950s brought about the rise of the modern computer, and with it the study of how these machines parallel human thinking. In the most basic way, computers take in information, process it internally, and then produce some observable product. Scientists and psychologists in the emerging field of computer science, such as Herbert Simon and Allen Newell, saw clear analogies between these intelligent machines and human thinking. Whereas human thought could not be observed, these new machines could be understood and designed so that the internal mechanisms and processes were explicit, manipulating symbols based on a logical system that processed information.[11]

Today, with much more sophisticated computers and the continual expansion and development of the Internet, information processing is no longer seen as an event that takes place in isolation. Instead of processing data locally on a single machine, a typical action on the computer involves gathering information from a range of sources, produced by many different people. It may involve using tools that are based in other locations, or artifacts produced on the other side of the globe. Essentially, we gather, process, and create data and information in interconnected ways, networked and embedded within many different entities.

Although one might not initially equate the museum-based experience of a group discussion of a Renaissance painting with a computer-based experience, the collaborative cognitive processes that are engaged through a situated model have some intriguing parallels. Most museums place great value on the direct encounter with the original object in their collection, which of course cannot be replaced by any other type of experience, computer-based or otherwise. But how can museums seize the power and possibility of collaborative learning that computers and the Internet facilitate, a process that has distinct similarities to the in-person dialogic model, and even discover ways to augment and complement the in-person experience?

Situated and Distributed Cognition

The theory of situated cognition posits that human cognition and knowledge do not reside inside the mind of individuals in isolation. Rather, cognition and knowledge are inextricably connected to the body, to society and the environment, and even to artifacts with which we interact. By definition, knowing is not separate from doing, and is always dependent upon context. So rather than a focus on the individual, situated cognition requires that we examine the relationships between the individual and other entities, and consider how this relationship is dynamic and can change over time. Instead of seeing expertise as residing within the mind of one person, expertise can be shared among many, and needed information can also be stored in non-human artifacts to be called upon as needed.[12]

An extension of the field of situated cognition, called distributed cognition, is perhaps the most radical approach of the cognitive field, positing that the mind "leaks out into the world," and encompasses features of the physical and social environment. Cognitive activity is distributed across people, situations, and environment. This notion has roots in dynamical systems theory, tracking cognitive activity and how it changes and fluctuates not only as the individual's internal thinking changes, but also as the environment and situation change.

The field of situated and distributed cognition has seen developments from Edwin Hutchins at the University of California San Diego, who studied navigation on ships in the 1980s, and the collaborative cognitive approach used by the various members of the crew. Through this cognitive ethnographic research, Hutchins observed that the essential outcomes of the ship's navigational process were not confined to one individual, but were the product of the interactions among several specialized crewmembers using a complex set of tools. Decision-making occurred not only at the individual level, but also at an organizational level, and even a larger cultural level. As people interact in culture, we are continually confronted by resources for learning, problem solving, and reasoning. As Hutchins states, "culture is a process that accumulates partial solutions to frequently encountered problems. Without this residue of previous activity, we would all have to find solutions from scratch. We could not build on the success of others. Accordingly, culture provides us with intellectual tools that enable us to accomplish things that we could not do without them."[13]

All of the above theoretical frameworks from diverse disciplines can be helpful lenses through which to examine the philosophical and practical value that online collaborative learning can offer. Whether we are viewing our online collaborations through the vocabulary of digital literacies, or cognition, or learning theory, we believe that the educational potential of learning together online is exciting and immense.

SOME CHALLENGES TO COLLABORATING ONLINE

We believe that online collaborative learning has many advantages—practical, educational, philosophical, and that museums and their visitors can benefit from these new ways of working together. However, there are some challenges and issues that every museum should consider as it embarks on any project or program that invites online collaboration.

How Does This Support Our Mission and Goals?

Technology can be a fascinating realm to explore, especially with all of the new platforms and possibilities that are now available. But it is important to keep in mind that any type of online collaborative program or project, just like any other museum-based activity, should be in support of the institution's larger mission and goals. As you examine what you want to achieve in your institution, we hope that online collaborative learning may be an asset to help support your goals. But in some instances, it may not be. For many museums, the in-person encounter will take priority.

A Precious Resource: Time

Perhaps the greatest challenge of online collaborative learning is that it can require a resource that is constantly in short supply—time. Although online collaborative learning invites, and requires, participation from all involved, the museum as originator and facilitator of any online learning project will need to devote time and careful attention to its creation, maintenance, facilitation, and long-term life. Also, as we will explain in the following chapter, the nature of collaboration itself takes time—often much more time than going it alone.

Trust

In a truly collaborative endeavor, you are embarking on new terrain. While the program or project may have a clear goal or purpose, change will occur. Participants may come and go. Often responsibilities and authority are shared. When working with individuals and other institutions, a high level of trust and mutual respect is needed.

So, Why Bother?

We believe that museums and cultural institutions can be leaders in online collaborative learning through their unique collections, expert staff, social spaces, and visitor-centric values. Museums, often seen as places where creativity and innovation flourish, can also be welcoming climates for learners of all types to come together and experiment. As we will explore in the chapters and case studies in this book, online collaborative learning can also inspire new ideas, can help solve practical problems and tap underutilized resources. Further, online collaborative learning can be a way for institutions to shift from being teaching institutions to learning institutions.

• • • Case Study

In the following case study, we learn about a successful collaborative education program conducted by Helena Carmena, manager of Teacher Services, California Academy of Sciences, and Emily Jennings, museum educator, the de Young Fine Arts Museum of San Francisco. The two institutions have been working together for several years to integrate the fields of art and science in working with 4th-grade students and their teachers. But as these two institutions build on their successes, they are also beginning to consider how their work might be communicated to others, and how new technologies could support or even expand their work.

Endnotes

1   A well-known example of this type of online collaboration is the story of the origins of the Web browser Mozilla Firefox, which was created by Blake Ross, a 19-year-old Stanford University sophomore, and Ben Goodger, a 24-year old from New Zealand, worked collaboratively through open-source code and collaborative platforms to create the browser that took the Internet world by storm in 2004.

2   Palloff, Rena M. and Pratt, Keith. *Building Online Learning Communities: Effective Strategies for the Virtual Classroom*, Wiley, 2007.

3   U.S. Department of Education. "Evaluation of Evidence-Based Practices in Online Learning: A Meta-Analysis and Review of Online Learning Studies," September, 2010.

4   Weil, Stephen, "From Being About Something to Being For Somebody," in *Making Museums Matter*, Smithsonian Institution, Washington, D.C., 2002.

5   Dewey, John. *Democracy and Education*. The Free Press, 1916.

6   Piaget, Jean. *The Origins of Intelligence in Children*, International University Press, New York, 1936, and Vygotsky, Lev, *Mind in Society: The Development of Higher Psychological Processes*, 1978.

7   McLuhan, Marshall, *Understanding Media: The Extensions of Man*, McGraw Hill, 1964, republished by MIT Press, 1994.

8   Jenkins, Henry, *Convergence Culture: Where Old and New Media Collide*, New York University Press, 2006.

9   Shirky, Clay. *Here Comes Everybody: The Power of Organizing Without Organizations*, Penguin Press, 2008, and Friedman, Thomas L. *The World is Flat: A Brief History of the 21st Century*, Farrar, Straus and Giroux, 2005.

10 Ashcraft, Mark H. and Radvansky, Gabriel A. *Cognition*, Pearson, 2010.

11 Newell, A., Shaw, J.C. and Simon, H.A. "Elements of a theory of human problem solving." Psychological Review, 65, 1958.

12 Robbins, P. and Aydede, M. *The Cambridge Handbook of Situated Cognition*, Cambridge University Press, 2009.

13 Hutchins, E. *Cognition in the Wild*, MIT Press, Cambridge, 1995.

WHERE WE MEET: A Case Study Integrating Art and Science

By Helen Carmena and Emily Jennings

Introduction

In a dimly lit room, 24 fourth-grade students sit intently, studying spot-lit tropical plants placed on four separate lab tables. The students pay particular attention to the relationship between light and shadow, noticing how some waxy leaves create glistening highlights, while other leaves overlap, creating deep dark shadows. Closely observing the plants is the first step in solving a larger challenge. The students must translate their observations to paper without the use of pencils and erasers. Instead, these students work with four sheets of construction paper, scissors, and glue.

Having just observed the lesson demonstration, the students clearly understand the goal of the project. Nonetheless, within five minutes of working with the materials, hands start springing up. Confronted by the uncertainty that accompanies all creative thinking, the students ask for further clarification about how they *should* create their compositions. In response to these questions, the teaching artist brings the lesson to a complete stop. With all eyes on her, she openly admits that she does not have the answer. She explains that artists, like scientists, constantly work with dilemmas that are ripe with potential solutions. Finding the answer requires the integration of experience and background knowledge. This brief narrative, which recounts the explicit cultivation of creativity through the demonstration of cognitive skills, lies at the heart of the following case study.

Background

This valiant student-centered discovery was part of an eight-week investigation into art and science integration. The project was a collaboration between two distinguished museums in San Francisco, the de Young and the California Academy of Sciences.

The project was one of many "Museum as a Classroom" (MAC) initiatives designed to investigate a range of topics with the assistance of student participants. The MAC project has a long history at the Academy of testing educational techniques, such as using scientific dichotomous keys, creating exhibits for students, and developing new classroom kits, including the skulls and owl pellets kits. In the fall of 2008, the MAC Project was on its eighth iteration when the Academy joined forces with the de Young. Compared to the discipline- or collection-specific frames of previous MAC projects, we strove to investigate a new teaching pedagogy that focused on the overlap of art and science. Integrating these subjects required a cross-disciplinary approach that was the true test of collaboration, joining two disciplines and two very different organizations. This format allowed the creation of the *Where We Meet* curriculum, now in its second iteration. In this case study we will trace the development, implementation, and refinement of the program.

The California Academy of Sciences is a natural history museum, planetarium, aquarium, and research institution. Its unique 150-year history and focus on research makes the organization what it is today, a highly respected scientific institution with a mission to explore, explain, and protect the natural world. Rigorous, accurate research and education are at the very core of this institution. The opening of a new building in Golden Gate Park in September 2008 marked the reinvention of Academy Education.

Upon returning to Golden Gate Park after a four-year hiatus in downtown San Francisco while its park facility was rebuilt, the Academy became a top fieldtrip destination for teachers and students in the Bay Area. Due to this exciting reopening, the Academy's Education Division was poised to engage with the educational community on a new level.

The de Young is an equally prominent neighboring institution. In conjunction with the Legion of Honor in Lincoln Park, the de Young is managed under the administrative umbrella of the Fine Arts Museums of San Francisco (FAMSF), the city's largest cultural institution. The De Young Museum was established in 1894 by M. H. de Young, publisher of the *San Francisco Chronicle*. The museum's collections include Pre-Columbian art, textiles, American art, modern art and photography, contemporary craft, and the arts of Oceania and Africa. In the fall of 2005, the de Young reopened after a five-year building project, and now serves as a popular community resource for San Francisco and the broader Bay Area.

While supporting scholarship in two distinct disciplines, the institutions are philosophically connected in many ways. The Academy's Education Division aims to inspire curiosity in students and teachers and to foster environmental stewardship and sustainability. Due to the educational shift after the introduction of federal legislation known as *No Child Left Behind* (NCLB), subjects such as science and art were de-emphasized, resulting in less content instruction in elementary schools. The Academy hopes to increase the quantity and quality of science instruction in the classroom, improving students' science performance and nurturing the next generation of scientists, science enthusiasts, and science advocates.

Similarly, NCLB impacted FAMSF's educational programming. Aware of the increased accountability surrounding fieldtrips, and in an effort to partner with classroom teachers, all the de Young's school programs are crafted in support of the California state content standards for visual arts, language arts, and social studies. The museum's interdisciplinary units employ student-centered inquiry techniques empowering students to engage directly with the process of interpretation and art-making. These units serve as a model for best teaching practices, as well as a catalyst for the further integration of core content areas. Through its curriculum efforts, the de Young strives to inspire lifelong learners who view the museum as a place to learn about themselves and the world they inhabit.

Design, Participants, and Development

Where We Meet grew from a kernel of an idea: to reinvigorate the learning experience with an explicit focus on creative thinking. As we developed the program, we articulated our primary goals, which included:

- Building a model that rigorously and authentically integrated art, science, and literacy, both in the museum and the classroom.
- Developing student skills of observation, communication, interpretation, critical thinking, and investigation.
- Researching student's perceptions of art and science.

The planning of this program also coincided with San Francisco Unified School District's unveiling of its 21st Century Initiative. This initiative would launch an innovative program that included training teachers to focus on investigation, communication, and other relevant skills needed to help students find success in the global society of the 21st Century. The initiative strove to expose students to the arts, sciences, and technology, thereby advancing career preparation, language development, and student engagement and achievement.

To create the most rigorous and authentic integration model, we surveyed the California state content standards in art, science, and language arts. After reviewing the potential connections, we structured the *Where We Meet* curriculum around the theme of light. As science and art educators, this theme provided the natural integration we hoped to achieve and offered students a unique and often overlooked lens for studying both disciplines.[1]

When developing our lessons, we incorporated journals to advance students' comprehension and literacy skills. Moving between both museums and continually encountering new content, the journals become familiar orientation tools where students could record information and reflect on the lessons they learned over the course of the series. Each lesson, and subsequent journal entry, started by defining the skills to be used and the new vocabulary required to understand the content. The journals effectively promoted student engagement, reflection, and retention, as well as providing an invaluable data source when we evaluated student learning. Through the development of the lessons and journal activities, we explicitly articulated five creative thinking skills: observation, communication, interpretation, critical thinking, and investigation. During each lesson, students defined and then used two to three of these skills, promoting both a mental and physical understanding of the concept. By working with each skill in an art and a science context, students also gained the ability to identify the similarities and differences in the two disciplines.

While working towards our three central goals, we also kept in mind a number of concerns. Foremost, we worked to ensure that the program reflected the equal integration of art and science. To challenge ourselves as planners and reinforce the students' understanding of the interconnections between artistic and scientific inquiry, we purposefully planned art activities that took place in the science museum and science activities that took place in the art museum. When asked to comment on the program, one student stated, "I learned art and science are connected, and you could use science to make art, and you could use art to make science." Another student commented, "Science and art both have creativity in them." These students' ability to identify the shared characteristics of both domains speaks to the potential of interdisciplinary learning promoted by the *Where We Meet* curriculum. Yet while striving to achieve our stated goals, we never let the real world application of the program drop from sight. We understood that using the simplest of means possible would ensure the overall success of the curriculum.

To pilot the *Where We Meet* curriculum, we selected a fourth grade class from a public school in San Francisco. With an almost even balance of girls and boys, the class represented the diversity of San Francisco Unified, both in terms of demographics and achievement scores. The overall make-up of the class provided a viable "lab" for experimenting with the *Where We Meet* lessons. After implementing the entire curriculum and analyzing our findings, we presented our research to the larger education community in August of 2009. During this presentation, we shared our findings regarding student perceptions of art and science, and the student narratives. The data revealed that after participation in *Where We Meet* many students' stereotypes of artists and scientists disappeared, such as all artists wearing berets, scientists only working indoors, and certain gender biases. However, these misconceptions were not fully addressed throughout the curriculum and could be further analyzed. The evaluation also brought to light the need to identify students that have a lack of confidence in art or science and to nurture their curiosity to build their morale in these subjects. Overall, the students showed a strong connection to the 21st Century Skills addressed in *Where We Meet* and the journals were a successful tool in the classroom and museum setting. The members of the school district were impressed by our research, which in turn sparked a fruitful collaboration with the San Francisco Unified School District.

Fig. 1: At the start of each session, students reflected on the previous week's skills by explaining how they used these concepts in their daily lives.

The formal support of the school district led to an exciting growth spurt in the fall of 2009. The district recognized that the *Where We Meet* curriculum—with its wealth of student data and rich piloted content—gave traction to the "21st Century Learning Initiative." However, the model of a staff-led, eight-week museum experience was not sustainable. The curriculum needed to be transformed into a version that teachers themselves could deliver after an in-depth teacher training. Condensing the original eight lessons into four, the curriculum team created an instructional sequence intended for the classroom. The design also included onsite lessons intended for the one-day fieldtrip to both the de Young and the Academy of Sciences. The refined lessons focused on looking closely, decomposition, exhibit design, and investigation. We also continued to highlight career options associated with art and science, such as naturalists, conservators, designers, and journalists.

Fig. 2: Students analyzed how artists use color to create a mood in a work of art. Using these ideas, they then generated an interpretation about the piece, which they communicated to their classmates.

In the spring of 2010 we piloted the refined lessons, gathering additional student and teacher feedback to ensure that the curriculum made sense and had a natural flow. Eagerly, the San Francisco Unified School District identified two schools to target. Our team of educators from both institutions ultimately served 120 fourth and fifth graders, teaching the lessons and modeling the program for the teachers. We received positive feedback and made additional adjustments to the content and structure of the curriculum to maximize student understanding and classroom time. In the fall of 2010, the curriculum will be offered to upper elementary teachers through a teacher training program designed to orient teachers to the lessons, provide art and science background knowledge, and discuss the use of light in both museums.

Fig. 3: Investigating color, from a scientific perspective, and learning the importance of color in living organisms.

How Does Working Collaboratively Add Value?

Working collaboratively produced radiating effects that shaped every aspect of the *Where We Meet* curriculum. These effects ranged from the program's nascent conception shared by two educators to the refined development of a sustainable professional development series that incorporates representatives from three organizations, the de Young, the Academy, and the San Francisco Unified School District. Working collaboratively added to the project in three major ways. It added excitement and energy to the development and implementation of the program, promoted levels of reflection not habitually practiced when managing programs in isolation, and stretched our individual and institutional resources, creating a program that far exceeded existing curriculum initiatives at either museum.

Like most productive collaborations, planning the *Where We Meet* curriculum required a large time investment. Contrary to most collaboration, this perquisite never hampered the development of the program, due to the synergy and excitement shared by the program developers. Throughout the process, we found new and exciting angles for exploring the content of our own collections, ranging from mixing colors to match those on tropical fish to appreciating the time scales that conservators consider when caring for objects. The enthusiasm and support of the participating students and teachers also added considerably to our sense of purpose and overall commitment to the program.

Throughout the 2009 and 2010 pilot stages of the *Where We Meet* curriculum, the program developers, in collaboration with the teachers, students, and eventually administrators, carefully reflected on the goals and aims of the curriculum. This level of reflection ensured that the program achieved its stated goals and produced nuanced research findings detailing student learning outcomes.

Our shared enthusiasm for the program also stretched our professional capacities. As discussed by Lester and Evans (2009)[2], collaborative praxis prompts individual growth, diminishes burnout, and increases the quality of scholarship. By working together we leveraged our professional and institutional assets, which included content experts in the areas of object conservation and biology. We also shared resources, such as working with program evaluators and teaching artists. In future iterations of the curriculum, this collaborative model will support teachers as they develop their own integrated lessons, thereby expanding the community of learners that now support the program. To share these resources with the broadest audience possible, we are now exploring how technology can support the integrated and collaborative core of the curriculum.

Next Steps: Using Technology To Support and Deepen Collaboration

Technology presents the opportunity to offer the curriculum online and deliver teacher professional development on art, science, and literacy integration on a grander scale. It also makes it possible to collect resources and capture experiences online so that they have a lasting and meaningful future. Transforming this project into a sustainable model of integration would involve expertise and resources from outside the two institutions.

Through networking and connecting with other institutions, the collaborative nature of this project continues, with plans to offer online and onsite courses on science and art integration with the Metropolitan Museum of Art and the American Museum of Natural History in New York City in the summer of 2011. The culmination of a joint online learning community can enhance the involvement of teachers across the country, expand the number of resources available on art and science integration, and amplify the national, pedagogical shift toward a 21st Century Skills initiative.

As cultural institutions, technology is an important tool for reaching our teacher audience. The Internet has two huge implications for education: a robust platform for finding information and an interactive tool for connecting people with similar interests. With help from our colleagues at the Metropolitan Museum of Art and the American Museum of Natural History, we will deliver an onsite/online course that provides a model of authentic art and science integration using 21st Century Skills. Educators will interact with each other online and develop integrated lessons that relate to museum collections. Through digitized collections and media, teachers participating in the course will have access to a wealth of museum resources for use in the classroom.

This summer we plan to connect teachers from the East and West Coasts online to create a community around 21st Century integrated curriculum. We hope that the participants will explore and examine 21st Century Skills, such as evidence-based reasoning and creative problem solving. Through this process participants and facilitators will come to understand how these skills are equally reflected in the practices of artists and scientists. Throughout the course we plan to assess the success of the format by investigating how the educators' needs are met. This foundational research will help inform future collaborative work between the four institutions and will provide a framework for authentic integration and collaboration.

Endnotes

1 Our lessons included the following topics:
   - Looking closely: sketching a specimen and an imaginary environment
   - Exhibit lighting in both the de Young and the Academy
   - Use of color in nature/color mixing
   - Importance of light energy/shadow and form
   - Use of color in galleries/natural pigments/chromatography
   - Decomposition/light penetration/construction paper investigation
   - Decomposition composition

2 Lester, Jessica N. & Evans, Katherine R. (2009). Instructors' Experiences of Collaboratively Teaching: Building Something Bigger. *International Journal of Teaching and Learning in Higher Education,* 20 (3), 373-382.

• PART TWO: Creating a Climate for
• Online Collaborative Learning

Online collaborative learning can take many forms. It can range from a blended learning course involving 20 participants to an online multi-institution conference involving 200 or more. But no matter what form online collaborative learning takes, there are some key factors, or ingredients, that can increase the likelihood of success. Some of these factors are very concrete and tangible—such as the tools one might need to collaborate online. Other factors are less tangible, but equally important, such as trust, respect, and a willingness to take risks. But before examining these key factors, it is important to consider whether collaboration is the mode in which you need to be working.

• • • Ways of Working: Are We Always Collaborating?

Sometimes collaboration is not required in order to achieve your goal. Sometimes, rather than collaborating, people and organizations can work together in other ways—and sometimes they decide not to work together at all. A collaboration that truly builds on everyone's contributions and ideas can be difficult, and collaboration done poorly can be less useful than not attempting to collaborate at all.

People can work together, and relate to one another, in very different ways, and at different levels. As you consider what it might truly mean to collaborate, you should also examine the other ways that people can work together. Here are the "5 C's" of how people (or even organizations) can relate to one another:[1]

COMPETITION

We have all experienced competition in some form or another, and sometimes in organizations this can even be mistaken for collaboration. Some work and management models posit that best outcomes come about through competing entities. In our contemporary culture, competition is rewarded, and it can be difficult to think outside of this model. However, in the end, competition is often about win/ lose relationships, and the entities are often operating with their self-interest in mind—not for the benefit of the public at large.

CONSULTATION OR CONNECTION

This is about the ability and/or willingness to share our learning, experience, and expertise with others as a way to assist their planning efforts. Rather than working exclusively within one's boundaries, it can allow for communication and some mutual support. However, consulting or connecting with one another does not guarantee that people will collaborate.

COOPERATION

Through cooperation, we recognize our common interests and values, and we determine a way to work together. We can still retain our separateness, autonomy, and viability. This can sometimes involve stating or formalizing an agreement that serves our respective needs and ensures non-competition. Through cooperation we might be able to balance our goals with the goals of others, but still retain our autonomy.

COORDINATION

Coordination means that we are consciously taking into account the activities of others when we are developing our own work and activities. This is about understanding the value of defining our "niche" and working with others to provide a continuum of services to meet the broader needs of our target population. We develop relationships with others that we hope will ensure non-competition around our particular area of work, and we provide and expect the same from others. Coordination does not mean that we share other aspects of our work, or even all of our resources. Coordination sometimes includes the sharing of physical spaces or assets. Coordination does not necessitate a shared interest in aligning and maximizing the results of both activities, a key element of any collaboration. Success is up to each individual part, and the greater, combined success is not a primary goal.

COLLABORATION

This means that we are truly coming together as separate entities to accomplish a common goal or purpose. This common goal can be better met through a collaborative process that brings together key stakeholders than through the efforts of a single entity. In other words, more can be achieved together than separately. We set aside the tendency toward turf protection, and each individual or agency commits its resources and expertise.

A useful table to examine the differences between these ways of relating can be seen here:[2]

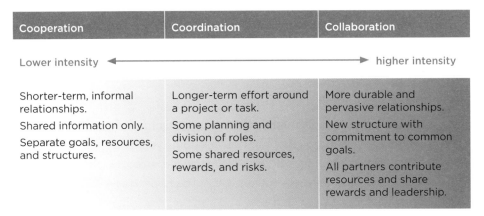

Cooperation	Coordination	Collaboration
Lower intensity ⟵⟶ higher intensity		
Shorter-term, informal relationships. Shared information only. Separate goals, resources, and structures.	Longer-term effort around a project or task. Some planning and division of roles. Some shared resources, rewards, and risks.	More durable and pervasive relationships. New structure with commitment to common goals. All partners contribute resources and share rewards and leadership.

True collaboration requires a commitment to shared goals, a jointly developed structure and shared responsibility, mutual authority and accountability for success, along with the sharing of resources, risks, and rewards.

● ● ● The People

Before considering the tools, the digital assets, the instructional design and factors; the most important ingredient in any online collaborative learning is people. Who will be collaborating, and toward what end? Who are the key stakeholders from your museum? Who will be involved from another museum or organization? Who else could be involved—teachers, students, parents, teens? As you consider who the key collaborators could be, you will want to consider their particular skills and strengths, why they may want to collaborate, and any potential barriers to their collaboration.

Although online collaborative learning has a particularly democratic, flat structure in which everyone can contribute, this doesn't mean that collaborators are without roles. It is important to consider what role each collaborator will play, what they can contribute, and how they may connect with others. The next chapter will focus on roles, including the role of the educator or leader.

The Climate for Collaboration Online: Some Key Factors

Similar to an in-person collaboration, there are key factors that must be in place in order for successful collaboration to occur. It is hard to over-emphasize exactly how important these factors are. In fact, these are all factors that do not materialize instantly. They require much thought and commitment, and must be shared among all of the collaborators.

THE EDUCATIONAL PURPOSE OR GOAL

Before considering if online collaboration in some form might help meet your needs, you should closely examine your educational goal. What are you hoping to achieve? What would success look like? What are some concrete outcomes that you hope to see? As you consider your educational goal, and also the possibility of using online collaboration as a means to achieve this goal, you should also consider the alternatives. What could you achieve in-person? What are the rewards and limitations of working together in-person, or online? And because any type of collaboration, in-person or online, can be time-intensive, what is the hidden cost? In other words, what will you not be able to do if you are dedicating time and resources to a collaborative project or program?

As you cast a critical eye on your educational goal, we encourage you to also examine how online collaboration could support, improve, expand, or deepen the educational encounter in some way. Could people be involved who otherwise wouldn't be able to contribute face-to-face? Are there aspects of working together online that provide distinct advantages to the in-person work? Although the cost in terms of time can be considerable, also consider how your program or project could benefit over the longer-term.

Remember, any collaborative project should clearly define a shared goal and purpose at the very beginning of the collaboration, with a genuine understanding of shared responsibility, mutual authority and accountability for success, along with sharing of resources, risks, and rewards. By setting goals, planning, and prioritizing, the collaborators should make agreements about the what, who, when, where, why, and how of the project. Each member of the team should also understand both the big picture and individual responsibilities.

A DESIRE TO INNOVATE, TO CREATE SOMETHING NEW

It is true that innovative solutions and ideas can come from individual insights and breakthroughs. But by working together and embracing the unknown, we can take risks, test, implement, and evaluate our ideas. When people influence others to collaborate in mutually beneficial ways, it often creates a place where innovation can thrive.

TIME

In many instances, we tend to forget how much time is needed to complete a project. It is often hard to quantify via a fixed-arrangement, such as two hours per week, when first embarking on an online collaborative learning endeavor. We have found that any given collaborative project can take at least a year to develop before involving the public. As with many programs, in the early planning stages it might take only few hours a month to begin to develop a program or project, but it could easily take 10 hours or more per week as the program intensifies.

MUTUAL RESPECT AND TRUST

In many cases, a collaborative project is seen as an experiment to begin with, and we need to understand that there is no existing path or formula to follow. We need to support each other, celebrate our successes, and respect each others' expertise and contributions, rather than focusing solely on our own tasks and responsibilities. Respect, trust, and confidence build over time.

FLEXIBILITY AND A POSITIVE SPIRIT

Innovation and creativity require quality time to think through options and opportunities. It requires flexibility to accommodate unexpected factors, challenges, and problems. When engaging in a collaborative effort, demonstrating a positive attitude will also serve as an essential component to the success of the project.

OPEN AND FREQUENT COMMUNICATION

The idea of open communication is not only to be clear about our intent, but also to follow through on what we say we will do. It includes soliciting feedback, encouraging others to play devil's advocate, and commending each other for proposing ideas that might be different.

A WILLINGNESS TO SHARE IN THE TASKS, RESPONSIBILITIES AND OUTCOMES

A successful collaboration depends on everyone's contribution. If participants do not contribute or share in a timely and regular way, then they could disrupt the progress of others. If working in different time zones and locations, it requires patience and persistence in returning and looking for the response. The very essence of collaboration rests on the premises of shared responsibility and collective accountability.

• • • The Means

As we stated in the preface, we will not devote a lot of attention to the tools themselves, as they change and evolve on an almost daily basis. However, it is important to consider the functionality of the various tools that are available—the advantages of each type, the costs, and the skills and training that are needed for each collaborator to feel comfortable using them.

There are number of categories of tools that you might consider when collaborating online. Here are a few:

Asynchronous Tools: Users may access these tools at any given time. Participants are not required to be online at the same time in order to engage in this Web-based activity. Participants contribute to the interaction on their own schedule, rather than at a specific time. An example of asynchronous interaction would be a threaded discussion.

Blogs: a dynamic online publishing system designed for two-way interaction by posting narratives and receiving responsive commentary. Examples: Blogger, Wordpress, LiveJournal.

Wikis: an online tool enabling users to add, remove, edit and change content remotely and collaboratively. Examples: pbwiki, Google Docs, Wikipedia.

Online Group and Social Networking: Web-based networking services that focus on building online communities of people who share interests and/or activities, or who want to explore the interests and activities of others. Examples: MySpace, Facebook, Yahoo Groups, Twitter, Ning.

Online Media Aggregating and Sharing: a website where users can upload, view and share different types of digital files such as videos, music, PowerPoint presentations, photos, etc. Examples: YouTube, Slide Share, Flickr, iTune, Voicethread.

Course Management System (CMS): a collection of software tools providing an online environment for course interactions; theses typically include a variety of online tools and environments, such as digital drop boxes for posting learning materials, a grade book, integrated email tool, chat room, threaded discussion board, wiki, etc. Examples: Moodle, Angel Learning, Epsilen, Blackboard/WebCT, Sakai.

Synchronous Tools: These tools allow participants to meet online on a given date and time to communicate and exchange ideas over the Internet, interacting with one another in real time.

Webinar Software or Services: a Web-based conferencing tool used to conduct live, collaborative and interactive, real-time meetings or presentations via the Internet. Examples: Adobe Connect, Elluminate Live, Microsoft Live, WebEx, Skype, GotoMeeting, Wimba.

Chat (online): a type of synchronous text messaging that instantly exchanges messages through an application via the Internet. Examples: Instant Message, Skype, Yahoo Chat.

Emerging Tools: 2010 New Media Consortium Horizon Report: Museum Edition states, "Increasingly, museum visitors (and staff) expect to be able to work, learn, study, and connect with their social networks in all places and at all times using whichever device they choose. Wireless network access, mobile networks, and personal portable networks have made it easy to remain connected almost anywhere."[3] With that, there are many potential applications on the horizon that might be integrated into online collaborative learning.

> **Mobile Media and Location-based Services:** a collection of software tools providing additional resources for reaching visitors and connecting the experiences that happen inside museums with those that happen outside. These include cell phone tours, mobile apps, ARG (alternate or augmented reality game connecting virtual and real experiences), or using QR code, two-dimensional matrix barcode readable by QR scanners using smart phone with a camera; encoded information can be text, URL, or other data.

Creating a climate where online collaborative learning can flourish is not easy. Besides the tools and key ingredients listed above, online collaborative learning requires patience and persistence. But with the support of colleagues and the institution, and with a sense of adventure, online collaboration can be a new way to interact with and learn from others.

• • • Case Study

In the following case study, Paige Simpson, Director of the Balboa Park Learning Institute, describes how the museums and cultural institutions of Balboa Park, as well as other organizations and colleagues in Southern California, came together, in-person and online, to conduct the recent Smith Leadership Symposium.

Endnotes

1 Mattessich, Paul W., Murray-Close, M., Monsey, Barbara R. *Collaboration: What Makes It Work*, Fieldstone Alliance, 2001.

2 Winer, Michale, and Ray, Karen. *Collaboration Handbook: Creating Sustaining, and Enjoying the Journey*, Fieldstone Alliance, 1994.

3   Johnson, L., Witchey, H., Smith, R., Levine, A., and Haywood, K., (2010). *The 2010 Horizon Report: Museum Edition*. Austin, Texas: The New Media Consortium.

BALBOA PARK LEARNING INSTITUTE'S 2010 SMITH LEADERSHIP SYMPOSIUM:
An Adventure in Blended Learning

By Paige Simpson

Background

The Balboa Park Cultural Partnership is a nonprofit organization through which 26 arts, science, and cultural institutions in San Diego's historic Balboa Park collaborate to achieve greater efficiency, innovation, and excellence. Member institutions vary in size and type and include museums of various disciplines, performing arts groups and theatres, cultural centers, gardens and the San Diego Zoo. Collectively, the Partnership's 500 trustees, 7,000 volunteers, and 3,500 staff serve more than 6.5 million visitors annually.

Fig. 1: Aerial view of Balboa Park1

Since launching in 2003, the Partnership has created a new way of doing business for its members by building a culture of trust, collaboration and sharing. Upon this foundation, members have been able to leverage their proximity and diversity to explore new frontiers in areas such as joint purchasing, communications, environmental sustainability, technology, artistic collaboration, and professional development. By strengthening member institutions, the Partnership seeks to transform the Balboa Park experience for visitors, build a vibrant and sustainable future for the Park, and increase the Park's value in the public and professional community.

One of the Partnership's featured programs is the Balboa Park Learning Institute, a collaborative professional education program for staff, trustees, and volunteers in arts, science, and cultural institutions. The Learning Institute leverages Balboa Park's unique setting as a learning laboratory to empower individuals and organizations with specialized, often "insourced" educational experiences that advance professional practices, build community, and promote innovation.

The Learning Institute was launched in October 2008 with a three-year, $500,000 21st Century Museum Professionals matching grant from the Institute of Museum and Library Services. In 2010, we served more than 2,300 people with over 45 programs. Many Learning Institute offerings are open to individuals and organizations outside of Balboa Park, as sharing is an important value of the Partnership. We also want to have our work contribute to a larger body of knowledge and practice across the cultural sector.

Issue

In accordance with other studies, the National Endowment for the Arts' report, *Arts Participation 2008: Highlights from a National Survey*, found that the number of American adults attending arts and cultural events has sunk to its lowest level since 1982. Understanding audience experience is imperative to increasing audience engagement and thus the community relevancy and future health of museums and other cultural institutions.

In response to this issue, the Learning Institute launched "Evaluating the Balboa Park Experience" in March 2010. In this 10-month professional development program, 20 staff from 12 Balboa Park museums and the

Balboa Park Visitors Center worked collaboratively with Dr. Marianna Adams (Audience Focus, Inc) to learn how to develop and implement a large-scale visitor survey. Participants represented visitor services, education, development, marketing, and the museum store from the following institutions:

- Balboa Park Visitors Center
- Japanese Friendship Garden Society of San Diego
- Mingei International Museum
- Museum of Photographic Arts
- Reuben H. Fleet Science Center
- San Diego Air & Space Museum
- San Diego Automotive Museum
- San Diego History Center
- San Diego Museum of Art
- San Diego Museum of Man
- San Diego Natural History Museum
- Timken Museum of Art
- Veterans Museum and Memorial Garden

Participants began by developing and testing a shared survey instrument. Over a 16-week period from May to September, staff, interns and community volunteers collected more than 10,000 surveys from visitors exiting the museums. From September through December, program participants worked with Dr. Adams and graduate students from the University of California San Diego to begin analyzing and presenting the data. Over the course of the program, participants completed up to 70 hours of professional development.

The audience survey focused on who is visiting Balboa Park museums, what motivates their visits, how they benefit from these experiences, and how else they spend their time in the Park. This was the first time Park museums engaged in collaborative audience research and the first time for several to conduct formal visitor research at all.

"Evaluating the Balboa Park Experience" was not just about teaching survey methodology. It was also about building community, shifting perspectives, and changing how the institutions work together to understand and improve audience experience. Although the staff representatives shared their new knowledge and experience with their institutions as the program progressed, this alone would not be enough to make a significant change. The Balboa Park community needed a shared learning experience that would reach more people, provide more context for the project and serve as a forum to debut the study publicly.

The Learning Institute's third annual Smith Leadership Symposium offered a prime opportunity for creating this shared learning experience. It would also take the Symposium—previously enjoyed by two hundred attendees as a free, half-day event with one keynote presentation—to a new level.

As planning for the Symposium began, conversations with leaders of the California Association of Museums (CAM), the California Exhibition Resources Alliance (CERA), and the Museum Educators of Southern California (MESC) revealed a mutual interest in the topic of audience experience, the speakers we were seeking—John Falk, Nina Simon, and Salvador Acevedo—and in our collaborative audience research project. Given this overlap and the challenging economic times at hand, we decided to leverage the work in Balboa Park and collaborate on the Symposium rather than creating duplicative programs.

SOLUTION

To create a program that met each of our needs, we drew upon careful planning, trust and goodwill, and a sense of adventure. Timing for the program worked out easily, so location became our first issue to tackle. Given the regional and statewide purviews of the partners, we needed to engage everyone's respective areas in this event—ultimately as much of the state as possible. While the group viewed the Symposium as ripe for connecting different areas through meaningful dialogue, we felt it was unlikely

Fig. 2: Smith Leadership Symposium at the San Diego Natural History Museum2

that people would travel to a single location (in this case San Diego) from across the state to participate. Thus, technology emerged as a practical strategy for implementing our program.

Fig. 3: LearningTimes' Jonathan Finkelstein working behind the scenes to produce the 2010 Smith Leadership Symposium.3

The only problem was, none of the partners had ever used technology to produce a program of this scale. The Learning Institute had the most experience given our partnership with the American Association of Museums (AAM) to deliver their webinars in a blended learning format (i.e., convening a group to watch the webinar together, complemented by an activity with a local expert on the same topic). So we called upon LearningTimes, AAM's technology partner, for help. Although a number of fears around the technology still existed, collectively we decided that this was the right opportunity to take the risk. We wanted to learn for the benefit of each of our organizations and to model for others the possibilities of integrating this type of online learning into professional development.

Our planning group expanded to include Cultural Connections of San Francisco, the Crocker Museum of Art, the Children's Discovery Museum of San Jose, the American Association of Museums, and San Diego Zoo Global. Together we wrestled with different scenarios for structuring the program, ultimately deciding to:

- Base the program live in San Diego at the San Diego Natural History Museum in the morning and the Museum of Photographic Arts in the afternoon.
- Host convening sites at the Museum of Contemporary Art in Los Angeles and the Children's Discovery Museum in San Jose.
- Connect all sites via a live, two-way webcast, which also allowed people unable to attend a site to participate online from wherever they were located.
- Utilize an online graphic facilitator to capture the proceedings in real-time drawings.
- Structure the morning with a keynote session in which John Falk, Nina Simon, and Salvador Acevedo shared 10-minute presentations highlighting their most recent work, followed by an interactive dialogue with attendees from all sites and online. This session provided the context for a second keynote in which the Balboa Park study was presented by Dr. Adams and Dr. Micah Parzens, CEO of the San Diego Museum of Man; Jennifer Telford, Director of Marketing, Reuben H. Fleet Science Center; and Amber Lucero-Criswell, Director of Education, Museum of Photographic Arts.
- Offer related breakout sessions in the afternoon at each convening site and for the online audience, and then reconvene virtually for a culminating session at the end.
- Charge for the event, with tuition discounts for membership affiliations and groups.
- Engage LearningTimes to create an event website, manage online registration and e-commerce, and produce the webcast.

With this planning in place, the Learning Institute's third annual Smith Leadership Symposium—"Motivations, Interactions, and Impact: Understanding Audience Experience"—began to take shape.

OUTCOME

The Smith Leadership Symposium was held with great success on Monday, November 8, 2010. Exceeding targets, more than 700 people participated—a sold out crowd of more than 200 people in San Diego, 120 in Los Angeles and San Jose, and 400 people from as far away as New

Zealand. The technology went smoothly, the dialogue was lively, the day's energy was momentous (we have already seen changes in practice as a result) and, throughout the process, our planning team learned a great deal.

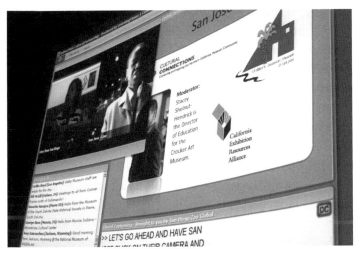

Fig. 4: A view of the online presentation of the 2010 Smith Leadership Symposium[4]

One learning curve was navigating the many partners involved in this collaboration. Although some had worked with each other previously, it was the first time we all had worked together. The pre-existing relationships became extremely useful, helping us to build trust and work effectively as an overall team rather quickly. This was particularly important since each site enacted a slightly different version of the program, creating many moving parts to implement. Also helpful was that we had been very upfront about the risks inherent in doing this program for the first time, and what level of risk the different partners were willing to assume.

Technology remained a learning curve throughout, fueling many of the unknowns and anxiety about the Symposium. What would happen if the webcast did not work? What if the sites lost connection? Would people like the multi-site format? To assuage these concerns, we conducted as much advance testing as possible. However, we had to accept there is always an element of "what if" until show time arrives. In Balboa Park, our prior experience with collaboration and technology through the Balboa Park Online Collaborative helped ease some of our community's tensions

PART THREE Roles and Routines: People and Time

Sharing information and ideas across thousands of miles, co-editing documents that result in new approaches, embedding the infinite resources and dynamic media of the Internet—all of these activities showcase the appeal, and the fun, of collaborating online. But beyond the bells and whistles of novel technological tools, and even beyond the bits and bytes of data and information, online collaborative learning is ultimately about one primary thing: people.

As museum professionals, we know this story well. Although we are surrounded by fascinating collections and objects, buildings, traditions and histories, ultimately the strength of any museum is how it engages with people and communities to create public value. As the great museum scholar Stephen E. Weil wrote, museums have shifted from being about something to being for somebody.[1]

It is beyond the scope of this book to do a thorough analysis of how people communicate and collaborate with one another in all types of environments or situations, in-person or online. The study of group norms, the development of teams, and the dynamics of people working together is a field in and of itself that engages wide-ranging disciplines such as sociology, psychology, organizational leadership and behavioral studies. It would not be possible to tackle all of these areas within the scope of this book. At the same time, it would not be adequate to write about online collaborative learning without discussing at least the basic premises of some of these fields of inquiry.

Individuals, Groups, Teams, Communities

At times, the best way to solve a problem or create something new is to work alone. When one works alone, decisions can come quickly, the process moves along at a rapid pace, and there is no need to await the input or decisions of others. Sometimes we need to make decisions autonomously and expediently, with little or no input from others.

But often we want or need to work together in a group or team. This can be for different reasons. Perhaps we need to solve a problem in a collective way, or we need advice or consultation from others, or we need to involve others in decisions in order to get their "buy-in" and support. Sometimes we also need to recruit the expertise of others in order to innovate and create something entirely new. In many museum settings, we are accustomed to working among others, and for others, within and across departments. Many of our projects and programs benefit from the collective efforts of a group or a team, and by working collaboratively, we also anchor our work more deeply in the institution.

As we all know well, working with a group of people does not necessarily mean that we are all working together on a team toward the same goal, or even that we are collaborating at all. We have all had the experience of being a member of a group, and suddenly find that we're stuck, not getting traction, or not communicating with one another. Unfortunately, online collaborative learning isn't always a solution to these dilemmas. In fact, collaborating online requires an even closer connection with fellow participants and colleagues. In order to acknowledge some potential hurdles or challenges when beginning to collaborate online, let's examine some of the basic concepts of groups and teams, and how these group dynamics work in online environments.

One of the often-cited pioneers of group behavior research is Bruce Tuckman. In the 1960s, Tuckman identified a number of stages of development that groups often encounter. Although these stages sometimes take different forms, the classic stages proposed by Tuckman are:

Forming: Group members get to know one another, discuss the problem or challenge at hand, and begin to forge relationships among group members.

Storming: During this phase, different ideas are competing for consideration, and also debate may occur about how the group will form decisions and what types of leadership are needed.

Norming: The goal or issue that the group will work collectively on is determined, and the competing ideas are set aside so that the group can focus on the issue at hand.

Performing: This stage, which is not always reached by all groups, is when the actual work begins to get done.

Informing and Adjourning: In this final stage, the group communicates its work to others outside the group, and makes agreements about how the group will continue, if it will continue at all.

Tuckman's model of group development[2] has been researched and applied extensively for in-person groups for several decades. However, the study of how groups work together collaboratively online is an emerging field. It also is dependent on the project or task at hand, the duration of the project, the means through which the group is communicating online, and whether the collaborators have contact with one another in-person as an added component.

Two researchers, David Jaques and Gilly Salmon, have developed a five-stage framework for e-groups[3]. This model emphasizes how the participants build both skill and comfort working together as they progress through each stage, and the model requires that the teacher, or e-moderator, facilitate a structured process and continual encouragement throughout the five stages.

The five stages of e-group development proposed by Jaques and Salmon are:

Access and Motivation: Individuals access the online environment, and are provided with basic orientation to the tools and the processes through which the group will communicate.

Online Socialization: This phase involves the individual group members forging their online identities and making connections with other members of the group.

Information Exchange: The participants communicate with one another, sharing information and ideas through online discussion, sharing links and files, and other types of online communication.

Knowledge Construction: At this stage, the work truly becomes more collaborative, as the participants are working together in a symbiotic way to build or construct processes and products that are of benefit to all in the group.

Development: This is the continuation of the previous stage, but the participants also seek out more benefits from the online collaboration, for themselves personally and beyond the course or project.

TEACHERS AND LEADERS

With such a horizontal, democratically organized structure in online collaborative learning environments, one is likely to ask who is taking the lead, or who is the teacher? In some online collaborative projects, it may not be necessary to have a teacher, per se. But in many, such as an online or blended learning program, having a skilled and active teacher is essential.

While it is not possible to provide a formula or recipe for effective teaching online in every situation with all types of learners, there are some characteristics and approaches that one should keep in mind. In many ways, these are not very different from the traits that an effective in-person educator possesses, but there are some differences.

Effective e-teachers do the following:

Create a Climate for Learning: Teachers and leaders in online collaborative learning create the structure in which learning is going to happen. Besides the activities or lessons that will unfold, the e-teacher or leader also needs to help build other elements that are less visible, such as mutual respect, trust, and community.

Helping to Establish Social Presence: Social presence is vital to online learning in any form. This involves the forging of online identities, and how these identities convey a sense of personality and community to others.

Encouraging Active Participation: Similar to in-person teaching, effective e-teachers encourage everyone to participate and contribute. This can be done by affirming contributions, doing regular check-ins, and being responsive when challenges arise.

Encouraging Others to Take Leadership Roles: Great teachers are also great delegators. Distributing tasks and responsibilities across the group is key, not only to share in the work and rewards, but also to tap into the interests and skills of each collaborator.

Shifting Roles and Sharing Responsibilities

In any type of collaborative endeavor, all the participants are actively contributing to the end result. Often it is useful to define each group member's role from the start: scheduler, note-taker, resource expert, or facilitator. However, when a group truly begins to function as a team and work in a collaborative spirit, these roles can shift and change.

Online collaborative learning can support, and even encourage, this shifting of roles. For one reason, all participants access the online environment and resources in an equitable way. With the exception of a leader's access to administrative functions of the technological tools, often there is no staging area, no "behind the curtain" hidden content, and no moment of "reveal." Instead, all of the collaborators access the same materials, use the same tools, and are working together to build and create.

Through this shifting of roles and responsibilities, one challenge that museums may find troublesome is the notion of shared authority. Often museums do not want to acknowledge that they are not the experts in a particular area, as they see their proper roles as pillars of public trust and a source of knowledge. Obviously, the museum cannot be an expert in everything, to everyone. Perhaps a better way to consider the roles of collaborators and the responsibilities they share is not one of hierarchies, but rather as co-experts.

COLLABORATORS: CO-EXPERTS WORKING TOGETHER

When we think about the phrase, "bring in an expert," there are probably some audible groans among our ranks. This phrase might conjure images of museums bringing in a consultant who has been asked to lend expertise, solve a problem, or at the very least, become a temporary solution to a problem.

As educators know, learners are not passive, empty vessels waiting to be filled with information from the teacher. In fact, learners come to any educational situation brimming with all types of experiences and information, and in a sense, they are operating as consultants: they bring in their expertise. All participants have their own types of expertise: a particular skill, language, interest, or experience in the world that informs the group's work and can contribute toward the solution.

We may not always consider learners, or fellow collaborators, to be experts. But when we consider that they are bringing their own skills and ideas to any given situation, we need to find ways to use that expertise and draw it out. Online collaborative learning can be a way for each participant to contribute his or her expertise through a new means that becomes visible to the entire group. This can be simply sharing information, reacting and responding, or reflecting and reviewing among fellow experts.

HOW EXPERTS THINK, AND HOW ONLINE COLLABORATIVE LEARNING MAKES THAT THINKING USEFUL TO THE GROUP

When we've been in the presence of an expert, such as a master teacher, sometimes it can be exciting — and also frustrating. Many of us have had the experience of studying with a brilliant teacher or professor who was completely immersed in his or her subject matter, but not able to convey it or communicate it to others. Cognitively, we know that experts may process information in ways that are different from other thinkers or novices. It can be very difficult for experts to "scaffold" the learning experience for others because, in fact, they have eliminated some of those necessary steps in their own thinking process.[4]

Online collaborative learning isn't a silver bullet to resolve the various ways that co-experts are thinking and processing information, but the act of bringing together experts of many types around a given topic or subject can harness ways of revealing new approaches to a subject or problem. Online collaborative learning is a way for experts — in all forms — to come together over time and present all of these perspectives, and make their thinking processes visible. It doesn't necessarily mean that by working together online all will become clear. In fact, sometimes divergent ideas are competing with one another, and a new challenge that arises is the process of sifting through all of the information that has become available to the group online[5]. But a key is that the collaborators, and the ideas that they are making visible, are all located in the same shared space, with all of the collaborators accessing and examining these contributions. And because of the flexibility and mutability of these technologies, it is possible to re-visit, to re-examine, to re-think all of these pieces many times, and over time.

CREATING A COMMUNITY OF PRACTICE

When practitioners, or co-experts, are brought together in a common space to work together over time, a particular type of community can be forged: a community of practice. With origins in medieval workshops and apprenticeships, this idea of a community of practice has received considerable research and attention in recent years. As people with common interests, professions, or goals come together and share experiences and information, the community of practice can not only develop its members personally or professionally, but members can also innovate and solve issues collectively.

Beginning in the early 1990s, the cognitive anthropologists Jean Lave and Etienne Wenger have spearheaded much of the research on communities of practice.[6] Communities of practice can take many forms, and can be formal or informal. In addition to supporting the professional development of the communities' members, Lave and Wenger also discovered that communities of practice, through their collaborative nature and the sharing of co-expertise, can support the communication of tacit knowledge, or information that sometimes is not easily articulated. Through communicating constant feedback from the members of the group, and through sharing information over time, this tacit knowledge can support innovative ways of solving problems.

THE IMPORTANCE OF BRINGING TOGETHER DIVERSE COLLABORATORS: BRIDGING SOCIAL CAPITAL

In addition to bringing together like-minded individuals, or even like-minded organizations, perhaps one of the greatest assets of online collaborative learning is its ability to bring together diverse collaborators — people who are quite different from one another. Of course, as the saying goes, birds of a feather flock together. But as author Robert Putnam argues in his book *Better Together*, social networks that include diverse stakeholders are essential for a healthy public life and society because ultimately they can lead to greater mutual understanding, locally and globally. Through the interaction of diverse individuals, or organizations, we can increase what Putnam defines as social capital: networks of mutual assistance and trustworthiness that not only help the members of the group, but also bystanders.[7]

TAKING TIME: THE WHEN OF ONLINE COLLABORATIVE LEARNING

Perhaps the greatest asset, but also the greatest challenge, of online collaborative learning is the resource that is often so limited in our schedules and in our organizations: time. As we work together in any group, in person or online, we find that our success is often based on the amount of time that we can dedicate to moving our efforts forward. Although we may sometimes see technology as a "quick fix" or a way to increase efficiency and communication, the reality is that online collaborative learning, in its most successful forms, takes as much time, or more, as in-person collaborations. It can require time to become oriented to the tools and online environment, to establish social presence and learn about the collaborators' working styles, and to establish momentum.

Some advantages can result when working over time. By working in spurts, either asynchronously or through multiple synchronous sessions, we can build slowly and methodically and build on small successes. Online technologies can allow us to access materials and tools at our own pace, and often on our own terms, as we collectively build and share.

When we work together online in a digital platform, we are also often gathering and accumulating materials, linking to external resources, and working in an additive process, rather than a subtractive one. So over time, we may be able to locate some surprises — a type of digital archeology that results in a "eureka" moment. Perhaps we can re-visit an idea or resource that was examined weeks or months ago, and see it in a different light. Or we can examine the feedback that we have gathered from participants, and over time, evaluate it in a new way.

Certainly working over long periods of time can be a challenging. Progress can be slow. In asynchronous online environments, such as a threaded discussion, conversation unfolds bit by bit, and it can take days or even weeks to feel as if a dialogue is emerging. It also can be challenging to make decisions over long periods of time, and especially if collaborators are working asynchronously. When this happens, it may become necessary to do regular check-ins by phone, Skype, or using a webinar platform so that decisions can be made.

• • • Case Studies

In the following two case studies, we learn about the power of online collaborative learning to bring together people who normally wouldn't be working together, and how, over time, the work of these diverse collaborators contributes to the knowledge of the organization and the public at large. First, we learn about the non-profit organization Global Kids, which brings together youth and museum experts from across the country, and across the world, to examine important global issues. Rafi Santo, Senior Program Associate, and Shawna Rosenzweig, Senior Trainer at Global Kids, tell us about their dynamic and innovative programs using technology in collaborative ways. Then, we hear about a year-long, in-person and online teacher professional development collaboration, Teach with O'Keeffe, led by Suzanne Wright, Director of Education at The Phillips Collection in Washington, D.C. Through in-person forums and online interaction, the collaborators learned more about their teaching practice, and also learned some lessons about how they might use technology in the future.

Endnotes

1   Weil, Stephen. "From Being About Something to Being For Somebody," *Making Museums Matter*, Smithsonian Institution, Washington, D.C., 2002.

2   Tuckman, Bruce W. and Jensen, Mary Ann C. Stages of Small Group Development Re-Visited. Group and Organization Studies, December, 1977.

3   Jaques, David and Salmon, Gilly. Studies of Group Behavior. Printed in Online Communication and Collaboration: A Reader, edited by Donelan, Helen, Kear, Karen, and Ramage, Magnus. Routledge, 2010.

4   Ericsson, K. Anders, Charness, Neil, Feltovich, Paul J. Hoffman, Robert R. The Cambridge Handbook of Expertise and Expert Performance. Cambridge University Press, 2006.

5   For a discussion of the dangers of "information chaos" see Kear, Karen. Collaboration via online discussion forums. Printed in Online Communication and Collaboration: A Reader, Edited by Donelan, Helen, Kear, Karen, and Ramage, Magnus. Routledge, 2010.

6   Lave, Jean and Wenger, Etienne. Situated Learning: Legitimate Peripheral Participation. Cambridge University Press, 1991.

7   Putnam, Robert. Better Together: Restoring the American Community. Simon and Schuster, 2003.

I DIG SCIENCE: USING VIRTUAL WORLDS TO PROMOTE TRANSNATIONAL CONNECTIONS

By Rafi Santo and Shawna Rosenzweig

Introduction

A teen, small pickaxe in her hand, stands over a large plot of ground marked by a grid of long, intersecting planks of wood. "Where do we think that leg bone I'm working on should go?" Her teammate responds, suggesting that the bigger legs probably go in the back of the fossil. One of the adults nearby suggests using Google to find a picture of what their animal looked like, in order to get the right configuration. Earlier in the day, these teens, along with others in their group, met with a paleontologist who fielded their various questions, such as why some herbivores evolved to be faster than their predatory counterparts, while others did not. Later they gather by campfires to work in small teams, debating the designs of their fossil exhibits, which would include their completed fossil, along with relevant research and photos to contextualize it. In the late afternoon, the youth log off and return home, some to Brooklyn, New York, some to the South Side of Chicago, while their paleontologist guide is likely already asleep at his dig's campsite, as it is almost midnight in Zambia by that point.

Even ten years ago these interactions among the participants would have been impossible, but today they are able to do all of these activities through online collaborative technologies. These technologies, thoughtfully integrated with the resources of a world-class museum and an innovative after-school organization, helped to create the *I Dig Science (IDS)* program, a space where youth have unique opportunities to develop leadership skills, scientific knowledge and identities as global citizens.

The program, currently with three iterations behind it, *I Dig Tanzania, I Dig Zambia,* and *I Dig Brazil,* features youth from multiple locales working together outside of school in the afternoons or during the summer months through a synchronous, persistent three-dimensional digital environment. They meet in a custom-designed online space, built using the Second Life virtual world platform, which allows them to engage in simulations of both scientific practice and contemporary human rights issues, connect with researchers doing paleontology field research on the other side of the world, and collaboratively create dynamic media content around what they are learning.

About Global Kids and The Field Museum

The organizations behind this program, the non-profit Global Kids, Inc., based in New York City, and the Field Museum in Chicago, came together to leverage distinct staff expertise and organizational assets to create this new model of learning for their youth. Global Kids, founded in 1989, is a youth development organization with a mission to transform urban youth into successful students, community leaders, and global citizens by engaging them in dynamic and content-rich learning experiences. Operating in both in-school and after-school contexts, Global Kids utilizes experiential and project-based learning methods to design programs for schools across New York City. The goal is to empower youth with knowledge that connects the global to the local, and provide skills that allow them to take action on issues important in their lives.

In 2000, Global Kids founded its Online Leadership Program (OLP), a lab within the organization that leverages emerging media technologies in innovative educational practices to support the development of 21st-Century Learning Skills. Over the course of its development, the program has been responsible for an impressive array of youth media projects, including international online dialogues and social media projects, youth-created video game design, and distance collaboration utilizing virtual worlds. This experimentation is driven by a number of core ideas: that networked technologies and the Internet have the potential to further the reach of youth voices, and that through these technologies youth can engage serious global issues while developing 21st-century skills and literacy.

The Field Museum, founded in 1893, is one of America's largest natural history museums and has a public education mission focused on the diversity and relationships in nature and among cultures. This mission is served through vast collections, ongoing research and public learning programs. The collections contain over 21 million items, including "Sue," the largest known Tyrannosaurus rex skeleton. Ongoing research programs on botany, anthropology, zoology and paleontology, among other areas, provide the museum with an active base of expert resources on contemporary natural science. And like many other museums, its public learning programs include but also go beyond exhibits to reach into communities, schools, and increasingly, the Internet.

COLLABORATING ONLINE TO EXAMINE GLOBAL ISSUES

The *I Dig Science* program is a synthesis not only of the distinct resources of Global Kids and The Field Museum, such as field researchers in international contexts and staff with expertise in virtual worlds and learning, but also of the respective organizations' learning goals. It integrates international affairs, cultural competency and social justice with paleontology, evolution and biology to create a cross-disciplinary educational experience.

This approach has a number of advantages for the learners. To begin with, a wider range of youth with distinct interests becomes involved in the program. Many participating youth in Chicago have come to the program through the Field Museum's existing education networks and bring interest in subjects like anthropology and biology. Youth from New York are recruited through Global Kids'

Fig. 1: Botanical Garden: *I Dig Science* participants travel to the Brooklyn Botanical Garden to compare plant species of the U.S, and Zambia.

networks and tend to bring interests in human rights and international affairs. Youth with varied interests and expertise are able to contribute meaningfully to conversations and projects within the program that relate to these interests, providing a form of peer-to-peer learning.

The synthesis of learning objectives that comes from this kind of cross-institutional collaboration also allows participants to understand the interconnections between complex issues across disciplines. A key objective of the *I Dig Science* program is to enable young people to look at global issues through the eyes of multiple stakeholders. Participants see themselves in new environments, eager to learn about the past and the present that surrounds them on their expedition. In one activity in *I Dig Zambia*, for example, youth learned about the delicate relationship between economics, agricultural practice, and human interaction with local wildlife in rural Zambia by looking at local issues through the eyes of paleontologists and Zambian farmers.

The activity focused on sustainable agriculture and animal poaching, both prevalent issues to be addressed when exploring how paleontologists work with the local communities around land use. When looking to land issues in Zambia, the relationship between Acacia trees, crops, and elephant poaching arose as key to understanding this scientist-community dynamic. To examine this, students worked together in teams on a

Fig. 2: Elephant Activity: Global Kids leaders participating in I Dig Zambia work diligently in Second Life to prevent an elephant from destroying their crops during an interactive workshop on sustainable agriculture.

farming simulation in which they planted crops on their piece of land in Second Life. After a short period of time, an elephant avatar, controlled by one of the facilitators, came in and began destroying their plots of land. Quickly students began collaborating to build fences around their crops to keep the elephants away.

However, this teamwork alone did not complete the challenge. In this experiment, the Acacia trees began to die. The teams of students had to now find new ways to keep access to the trees for the elephants to feed on the insects that otherwise kill the trees. At the same time, they still needed to protect their crops from being trampled. In this example, technology provides students with a means to interact with their virtual environment in a manner that not only allows them to come to a multidisciplinary understanding, but one that also necessitates working together to act proactively rather than reactively to balance a complex ecological environment. Creating a simulation in a virtual world enabled students to successfully engage in collaborative scientific inquiry and problem-solving.

Other activities in the program also directly fostered various forms of collaboration that connected the youth in the program with each other, as well as with scientists in the field, organizations across the globe, and members of their own local communities. To understand the impact of HIV/AIDS in Zambia, the participants in New York and Chicago learned about the efforts and strategies that local Non-Governmental Organizations (NGOs) employed to combat the disease's spread. In this instance, video technology set the stage for collaboration, between Zambian NGOs, the IDS scientists in Zambia, the IDS participants, and the Zambian young people in their community. Online video created by various partners brought multiple perspectives on this harrowing issue directly to the participants. In one, an IDS scientist explained to them how the HIV/AIDS epidemic is understood from a scientist's perspective. In another, they learned background information on how the disease functions, and in the final one they learned about a sports-based, community-action model aimed at HIV prevention popularized by Grassroots Soccer, a local Zambian NGO

Technology provided a very real context in which the program participants could learn about applicable ways in which HIV/AIDS is being combated. At the same time, they could think critically about which efforts may work to address issues related to the disease in their own communities. Based on examples they observed in the work of Grassroots Soccer, the participants worked in small teams to facilitate soccer drills that were used to educate their peers on HIV/AIDS: mistakes and risks taken by team members playing soccer incurred penalties (in the form of push-ups) for the entire team, a metaphor for how risky sexual behavior by one individual endangers the whole community. The Grassroots Soccer workshop modeled how collaboration plays out on both the macro and micro levels in the fight against HIV/AIDS, with NGOs, scientists and community leaders working together to develop prevention strategies, while community members collaborate on the ground to implement these strategies.

The final project for *I Dig Zambia* had the participants working in teams to create a museum exhibit that showcased the fossil they worked diligently to excavate and assemble. While this aspect of the program includes career-exploration components of professional work in museums, it also provides a final opportunity to continue the collaborative practices among the participating youth.

After receiving an introduction to how museum exhibits are created and assembled, the young people were given a plot of land in a virtual museum to create an exhibit that would house their recently excavated fossil. The youth were introduced to and then took on a number of interdependent roles required to create the various elements of a museum exhibit. In this space, students were able to choose an activity they were most interested in, whether writing and researching their fossil for exhibit text, creating an accurate and aesthetic exhibit environment, or building and assembling the fossil itself. The use of virtual worlds for fossil and exhibit assembly allowed for collaboration across a variety of areas, fostering many forms of learning in the same activity.

Fig. 3 (Top): SL: A Global Kids Leader works to put the finishing touches on the exhibit that will house his team's newly discovered fossil.

Fig. 4 (Bottom): Exhibits: A team of *I Dig Zambia* participants from New York and Chicago gather in front of their finalized fossil and its accompanying exhibit.

Key Points for Successful Online Collaborations

The first and most important lesson in forging a successful collaboration is to create a program that aligns with the respective missions and goals of the partnering organizations, and leverage the resources that each brings to the table. *I Dig Science* was a synthesis of resources from Global Kids and the Field Museum, from the involvement of field research-ers and content from the museum side to the expertise in virtual-world pedagogy and curricular development that Global Kids brought to the table. Although it would have been possible to leverage organizational resources without addressing the missions of both organizations, we kept our focus on creating a hybrid program that brought together science and global citizenship issues so that the youth left with a more holistic understanding of both fields.

The second lesson is to conduct early and intensive joint planning and preparation, and regular check-ins. Collaborating with two different sets of educators across sites is difficult work, and requires a high degree of coordination. In the planning phase, being as explicit as possible about the learning objectives for each institution, the pedagogical approach they are applying, and their limitations as staff will greatly affect the success of the project. During program implementation, we scheduled regular times for the educators to brief each other ahead of the sessions and do a post-mortem afterwards to assess the success of each activity and plan the next session. For an intensive summer camp across two sites, this level of planned and informal exchanges was essential to the success of each workshop. In each iteration of *I Dig Science,* the participating institutions learned more about how the other site operates, its work culture, and its larger goals.

The third is to know your technology, leverage its assets, and make sure your teams understand it, too. It was critical that those staff members with the most technological expertise work with their new colleagues to bring them up to speed. Dedicated training sessions for staff in advance of the program allowed "newbies" to get their feet wet and understand the features of the technologically mediated learning environment. While all parties involved didn't have the same degree of expertise in virtual-world technology, their increased understanding allowed smoother running on the program, and brought in new perspectives on how the technology could meet our learning goals. Experimentation with interactive media that facilitate new forms of collaboration allowed this program to be designed in ways that previously haven't been possible. Real-time, embodied collaboration and cooperation in simulations that were custom made for the program meant that participants from across the globe were able to work together in a space created specifically for their participation.

Fig. 5: Video Conf: Global Kids Leaders in New York City share a laugh with their peers in Chicago at the Field Museum during a group discussion.

Conclusion

Ultimately, *I Dig Science* broke new ground in terms of incorporating multiple forms of technology into a STEM-based curriculum, fostering teamwork across geographic locations and collaboration across fields of study to explore scientific and global issues. The youth themselves valued the experience greatly. One teen in the program remarked: "Participating in *I Dig Zambia* was the highlight of my summer. I had the opportunity to learn with not only my fellow participants in New York, but also with a group of teens stationed at Chicago's Field Museum. Before IDZ, I knew very little about archaeology and knew even less about Zambia! Collaborating with such an intelligent group of enthusiastic teens definitely enhanced my learning experience. I was surprised by how well I got to know the kids in Chicago, and the bond that I formed with them over just a few weeks. Through the virtual world 'Second Life,' we completed projects together and learned a great deal along the way."

The strategies and lessons learned through *I Dig Science* have much to offer other museums and informal educational organizations in terms of what learner-centered collaboration can look like in the 21st century. Cross-institutional collaboration allowed for broader participation from respective organizational networks, resulting in more dynamic experiences for participants who interacted with peers with differing expertise and interest. But none of this work is easy. Working with multiple partners means more opportunities for miscommunication and misalignment of goals. Working with cutting-edge technologies means investing in staff expertise, as well as taking risks. However, when partnerships come into alignment and new technologies are harnessed, the kind of 21st Century Learning Skills so often sought after by informal educational institutions can be developed in the young people they work with—and in the organizations that are crafting the programs.

TEACH WITH O'KEEFFE: DEVELOPING A NATIONAL ART AND EDUCATION COMMUNITY OF PRACTICE

By Suzanne Wright

Introduction

The constant drum beat: teachers must teach to standardized tests to meet federal and state mandates. The result: a narrowed school curriculum that often excludes more expansive, art-based approaches to learning. Museum educators, however, witness an alternative: arts integration. We regularly observe the power of arts integration to teach across the curriculum, hone 21st-century skills, and reach students via non-traditional methods that target multiple modalities.

All museum educators have seen teachers soak up museum resources and animatedly exchange arts integration ideas at teacher trainings in their museums. At The Phillips Collection, teachers often describe these trainings as "stimulating" and even as "transfusions." Teachers' evaluations also confirm how these professional exchanges can diminish classroom isolation, bolster teachers' confidence in arts integration and help teachers advocate for arts integration to their colleagues and administrators.[1] We continue to wonder, though: How could The Phillips Collection, a private, mid-sized art museum in Washington, D.C., deepen its impact on education through our work with teachers? To answer this question, we initiated a year-long experiment to create a national arts education community—both in-person and online—that would foster exchange about the power of arts integration and build a community of practice made up of teachers and museum educators.

About *Teach with O'Keeffe*

We began this experiment by capitalizing on the inherent national community created through traveling exhibition. While works of art frequently travel from one venue to the next, we wondered if school-based educators and museum staff might do the same—virtually, in-person, or both? In 2008, we launched *Teach with O'Keeffe,* which utilized the traveling exhibition *Georgia O'Keeffe: Abstraction* as the foundation of a community of practice around the theme of arts integration.

Teach with O'Keeffe involved three museum education departments—from each venue of the traveling exhibition—and a corresponding school partner in each community. In Washington, D.C., The Phillips Collection collaborated with two D.C. Public Schools: Peabody Early Childhood Center and Stuart-Hobson Middle School. The Georgia O'Keeffe Museum in Santa Fe, New Mexico partnered with the Turquoise Trail Public Charter School, and the Whitney Museum of American Art worked with the West Side Collaborative Middle School, an urban arts-integration public school in New York City. The 19 participating school and museum educators were able to travel to all three exhibition venues in person, and continued their exchange online. The program, which unfolded over the course of a year, encouraged the implementation of arts integration lessons, and through this approach, impacted over 500 students.

A Year-Long Exchange: In-Person and Online

The in-person forums, each lasting about three days, took place in New York (October 2009), Washington, D.C. (March 2010), and Santa Fe (June 2010). Our momentum and community grew during each of these in-person forums. In New York that fall, we began our conversation by learning about O'Keeffe's art and life, and also with an orientation to the online tools that we would use to continue our conversations during the year. In the spring in Washington, D.C., we focused on sharing ideas about how to integrate works of art into our teaching. Then in the summer in Santa Fe the participants developed advocacy strategies and tools.

Fig. 1: During in-person forums, museum and school educators delved deeply into the teaching benefits and challenges of arts integration.

During these in-person forums, we strove to bridge gaps in understanding between museum and school practices. As a group, we analyzed the different exhibition layouts, curatorial choices, and gallery interpretation. O'Keeffe educators met with museum personnel at each venue—from curators and conservators to communications staff—to better understand the inner-workings of exhibition development and museum culture. In this way, *Teach with O'Keeffe* hoped to reveal the museum's processes and possibly inspire museum-based school curricula. Also at each venue, the O'Keeffe educators visited the partnering schools where they met with students and saw their colleagues implement arts-integrated lessons. This equitable arrangement meant that all O'Keeffe educators shared their work in the context of their own culture and environment, lending authenticity to the project. Indeed, as early as the first forum, evaluation data indicated that 87% of O'Keeffe educators increased their understanding of their museum/school colleagues as a result of the initiative.[2]

Georgia O'Keeffe's artworks became a shared language that unified all of the participants, regardless of their geographic location. O'Keeffe's art served as a type of "control," which amplified similarities and differences in styles and approaches to arts integration. For example, O'Keeffe's cropped, close-up imagery spurred several viewfinder activities in which students looked through a small opening to select, eliminate and emphasize their subjects. At the first forum, the O'Keeffe educators experienced how the New York team used the holes in everyday objects as well as traditional rectangle viewfinders to engage their students in looking. In the heart of O'Keeffe country, inspired by their New York colleagues, the New Mexico teachers followed O'Keeffe's practice and literally raised animal pelvis bones to the sky to observe and photograph the beautiful blue shapes created in the voids.

Fig. 2: Teach with O'Keeffe coalesced into a national community of museum and school educators after a year of in-person and online exchange.

Teach with O'Keeffe was among the Phillips' first forays into online communities and communication. We knew that we might need to employ both synchronous and asynchronous tools[3] to enable the O'Keeffe educators to share ideas across geographic distances and within their busy schedules. Participants used VoiceThread to share their educational practices between the October and March forums, and the webinar platform Elluminate to have a live meeting mid-way through the project in January 2010. Each school team was required to create VoiceThreads, which are multimedia slideshows, illustrating their curricula as it was being implemented. These VoiceThreads showcased students' art-integrated work, the teachers' lesson plans, and photographs that documented the process over the year.

Evaluation: Seeing Evidence of Arts Integration and a Community of Practice

Evaluation findings distributed by Audience Focus, the independent firm who evaluated the project, indicate that O'Keeffe educators increased their skills and confidence teaching with arts integration and considered themselves part of a national *Teach with O'Keeffe* community. In a summative pre/post written survey, educators significantly increased their skills and confidence teaching with arts integration from September 2009 to June 2010. The number of educators who rated their arts integration skills as "high" rose from three in the pre-survey to ten in the post-survey. Confidence also increased over the course of the year: five educators rated their confidence with arts integration teaching as "high" in September, compared to 13 educators the following June.[4]

Similarly, 13 O'Keeffe educators rated the benefit of belonging to this national community as "high" in June 2010, up from five educators in the fall of 2009.[5] This vibrant exchange among the O'Keeffe educators increased throughout the year. After the first forum, one teacher stated: "Hearing successes and struggles from different teachers across the country is incredibly valuable for me … I already was inspired to change/add a few things to my classroom because of our conversations."[6] After the second forum, March 2010, 100% of O'Keeffe educators felt like they were part of a larger community, and 94% were developing relationships with colleagues.[7] Audience Focus researchers also observed that "O'Keeffe educators engaged in sharing stories about their schools and students, asking their colleagues pointed questions about strategies and lessons and actively participating in all of the hands-on activities."[8]

Some Lessons Learned—and Some Surprises

While *Teach with O'Keeffe* has been a very successful national arts and education community, we have had our stumbling blocks and have learned a great deal through the process. Much of our learning centered on the use of the online tools to build our community of practice.

Originally, we intended to use VoiceThread as a communication tool for teachers to both display and exchange ideas about their process. The teachers fulfilled their commitment to post VoiceThreads, but dialogue over VoiceThread was limited. Training, time commitment, and a clearer goals and objectives seem to be the elements that we will consider more fully in the future. Although we surveyed the O'Keeffe educators before the start of the project to gauge their comfort level with technology and trained them to use VoiceThread, those less familiar with technology expressed great frustration. In addition, we discovered during the project that the New Mexico educators were prohibited from accessing VoiceThread from their school; one of the New Mexico teachers had to upload all of the VoiceThreads from home.

While the O'Keeffe educators spent a great deal of energy creating their VoiceThreads, few of them left comments, which was interpreted as non-interest. One museum educator at The Phillips Collection, Paul Ruther, learned a great deal about the teachers' process by viewing VoiceThreads, but his online queries often went unanswered. It is remarkable to note that the O'Keeffe educators produced 14 VoiceThreads with a total of 371 slides that colleagues could comment on. That's a lot to view, let alone discuss! However, upon analyzing these VoiceThreads further, we found that about three-quarters of O'Keeffe educators viewed all of the VoiceThreads. Indeed, there was an average of 15 unique viewers—out of a community of 19 educators and a handful of colleagues—for each VoiceThread. So O'Keeffe educators were observing their colleagues' practices online, but they weren't recording many comments. The comments that were made provide a window into the possible benefits. For example, New Mexico fourth grade teacher, Catherine Hathaway, recorded on her VoiceThread that she adapted an activity that the New York teachers demonstrated at the first forum: "I borrowed this activity [having each student adopt an O'Keeffe artwork and work with it] from the lesson we saw at West Side Collaborative in October..."[9]

At the third forum, O'Keeffe educators brainstormed ways in which VoiceThread might have been more effective. Many educators had similar feedback about the importance of clear goals and objectives: "If we had a [VoiceThread] project we were working on, then I think there might be more incentive to use it" and "the expectation that it would just continue without specific benchmarks didn't seem to work."[10] While the Phillips allotted some staff time to the online community, the feedback and experience with *Teach with O'Keeffe* indicate that future projects should dedicate equal time to the technological aspect of a national community to ensure adequate support of "digital immigrants," and to focus and monitor the conversation. In follow-up conversations with Audience Focus, an interesting hypothesis also arose: Can you have a robust in-person community and a robust online community within the same project? Former Audience Focus evaluator Jeanine Ancelet concluded: "The activities and intimate settings experienced during the three forums certainly overshadowed and, perhaps in many ways, diminished the more distant and detached realm of the internet and VoiceThread. Had the participants not been exposed to such rich, personal, face-to-face experiences, we may have seen VoiceThread being used in a more active and enthusiastic way."[11]

Fig. 3: VoiceThread multimedia slideshows enabled Teach with O'Keeffe educators to share their curricula, process, and student work with colleagues across the country.

While VoiceThread didn't function the way we had originally intended, there were many unintended benefits. Audience Focus used VoiceThread to supplement their data gathering. At the first forum, O'Keeffe educators created meaningful concept maps, diagramming and describing their perceptions of arts integration. Evaluator Jeanine Ancelet then scanned the maps and created an evaluation VoiceThread. Through VoiceThread, Jeanine asked each O'Keeffe educator to clarify or deepen his/her comments on his/her concept map. O'Keeffe educators then responded, via VoiceThread, providing Audience Focus with much richer qualitative information. Audience Focus has continued to use VoiceThread as an evaluation tool to enrich its data collection with several projects.

It can be challenging to discover what actually happened in the classroom that resulted in some of the arts-integration projects. Teachers' VoiceThreads provided some of these missing links. We saw not only the projects but also the interim steps. We also didn't have to wait for months to discover how the teachers were implementing these lessons. Teachers posted them while the lessons were still fresh. We could ask teachers more focused and specific questions about their projects and process. Consequently, the VoiceThreads became a fantastic resource for refining the agenda for our January group meeting, articulating messages in our national Young Artists Exhibition in February, and developing the framework for the second and third forums.

The VoiceThreads also became a great promotion and advocacy tool that we shared with board members, funders and potential partners. In fact, "What is *Teach with O'Keeffe*?" — the only public VoiceThread — had a much higher audience of 475 unique viewers. Nonparticipants who were interested in the project could tap into the online community, including Phillips Collection trustees, who recorded comments on VoiceThread at a board meeting, weaving the Phillips leadership into the project and increasing their investment in the Phillips' educational activities.

Sharing Our Work with a Broader Audience, and Next Steps

The second half of *Teach with O'Keeffe* focused on exchange, dissemination and advocacy. At the March 2010 forum, the O'Keeffe educators presented to Washington, D.C. area educators. The Phillips also opened the *Teach with O'Keeffe* Young Artists Exhibition. Over 100 student artworks and cross-curricular projects from the three communities were publically displayed at the Phillips for about three months to demonstrate the power of arts integration. Concurrently, we launched an online version of the student exhibition with over 500 student works, thereby including every student who participated in *Teach with O'Keeffe*. The website enabled us to broadly disseminate examples of arts integration. In the first four months, there were over 75,000 hits to *Teach with O'Keeffe* student work online.

At the third and final forum in Santa Fe, much of the emphasis was on "transferability" and advocacy. The O'Keeffe educators considered how they might advocate for arts integration in their local communities, as well as regionally and nationally. They also began to develop an "arts-integration palette," a framework that teachers around the country might be able to use to enhance their skills using art in their curriculum.

We are now in the process of sharing *Teach with O'Keeffe* and vetting ideas for our next national initiative regarding arts integration. The O'Keeffe educators are presenting about the project at national conferences and are working on an arts-integration video and teachers' palette that we hope to share broadly to support the cause of art in education. We hope that we will create these national communities in the future. We have been very fortunate to receive funding from the Sherman Fairchild Foundation to support this work.

We will continue to refine our combined approach to communities with online forums and face-to-face meetings and interactions. This process of refining, selecting, and emphasizing reminds us of the words of Georgia O'Keeffe herself, who used these processes to locate "the true meaning of things." We hope our lessons learned from *Teach with O'Keeffe* will support your own collaborations at your institution.

Endnotes

1   Angelina Ong, Jessica J. Luke, Jacob Lawrence Project Evaluation: Final Report, Institute for Learning Innovation, 2008, p.17.

2   Marianna Adams, and Jeanine Ancelet, *Teach with O'Keeffe* Evaluation Reflections: New York Forum, Audience Focus, 2010, p.26.

3   I'm proud of myself for being able to use these terms with some fluency!

4 Marianna Adams, and Jeanine Ancelet, *Teach with O'Keeffe* Evaluation Reflections: Washington, D.C. Forum, Audience Focus, 2010, p.8.

5 Ibid. p.10

6 Ibid. p.26

7 Marianna Adams, and Jeanine Ancelet, *Teach with O'Keeffe* Evaluation Reflections: Washington, D.C. Forum, Audience Focus, 2010, p.8.

8 Ibid, p.8

9 Catherine Hathaway, Museum Project, http://www.VoiceThread.com (specific page not public). [accessed 10 January 2010]

10 Audience Focus, Santa Fe Forum notes, June 2010.

11 Jeanine Ancelet, e-mail message to author, September 8, 2010.

• PART FOUR Building Something New

Sometimes we work together collaboratively to solve an existing problem. By working collectively and sharing our ideas and resources, we can make an aspect of our work more efficient or more productive. Other times we work collaboratively to bring in a new voice or a new perspective, so that we can move forward in a way that simply wasn't possible before. Or at other times, maybe we're working together collaboratively because we have no choice: we have been assigned particular roles in our department or museum, and need to work together to arrive at some solution.

Many times, though, we collaborate because we want to create something new. There is a spark of wanting to create jointly, to innovate, and to produce something that we simply couldn't create if we worked independently. This spirit of wanting to forge our way into the unknown and to tackle a topic in a new way is really the heart of collaboration.

Collaborating online can be a spark, and then a support system, that generates and feeds this spirit of innovation and creativity. With new tools at our fingertips, and with new collaborators who are accessible to us whether they are down the block or on another continent, we can build, create, and share to our hearts' content.

• • • The Appeal of Making Things

For many of us, one of the great appeals of working in a museum setting is the fact that we are surrounded by objects that have been made by human hands: works of art, historical documents, scientific tools or instruments, or other products of material culture. We celebrate these inventions and innovations through our educational work, and we declare the continuing promise of these objects to our publics. In recent years, we have seen a rise in the popularity of creating things by hand. The DIY and Maker Movements, the proliferation of publications such as *ReadyMade* magazine and *Craft,* signal a time in our culture and history where we find significant satisfaction in the act of making and creating.

Perhaps it is the act of creating, and creativity itself, that hold such excitement and possibility for us as we build, whether in digital or analog form. Although the definitions of creativity vary widely, and educational theorists and psychologists often disagree about its elusive definition, one measurable facet of creativity that is frequently cited is the amount of divergent and convergent thinking that occurs during our creative process[1]. In divergent thinking, we generate many possibilities — we offer alternative solutions, we disagree and debate, and we expand and explore. In convergent thinking, we assess the possible solutions that have been generated, and locate the solution that may work best for a given scenario. In the online collaborative world in which we live, these creative thinking processes can happen continuously — and are encouraged — as we collectively shape and improve the digital world around us.

• • • New Ways of Creating the New

Although we all want to avoid the pitfalls of using technology simply for its own sake, and we maintain our focus on the goals that we want to achieve, it is also important to take a close look at the tools themselves. How can these new means of working and creating help us better understand what we might be able to accomplish? Not so different from artists seeking inspiration from new tools and materials, we should examine how these new tools and processes can support our work in new ways. One might think about the invention of tubes for oil paints in the 19th century, leading to innovative *plein air* painting practices, or in the 1960s when Minimalist sculptors looked to newly invented industrial plastics to make objects that were unique. How can we use our own new tools to work together in new ways, and to create new things?

The new tools that support online collaboration can enliven and expand a spirit of innovation. Our digital constructions are visible and tangible: they can be easily constructed from a variety of accessible and flexible tools. Our digital thoughts can be easily drafted, edited, shared and dispersed across collaborators and spaces, and also shared with the public, if we choose. Our digital constructions are dynamic in their form — visual, auditory, multimedia. And in the digital world we are able to continually construct in ways that are additive — that build and link to one another — rather than depleting resources or drawing from a finite pool of items. Similar to Michael Edson's description of a "commons" in the opening case study of this book, we are in a process of multiplying, rather than dividing.

Through this new means of communication and collaboration, we are inspired to innovate and create. This often happens with changes in technologies. For example, a project that has taken many forms over the centuries has been the pursuit of a universal encyclopedia of knowledge. Beginning with Enlightenment figures such as Denis Diderot, we saw the first forms of the encyclopedia as an attempt to capture human knowledge from a single or a few authors. In the 19th and 20th centuries, other innovators who built on the encyclopedia project drew upon recent innovations in technology, such as the index card, and later microfilm, in order to capture and communicate information to many. Recently, the best example of using new technologies for the encyclopedia endeavor is, of course, the collective creation of Wikipedia. Founded by Jimmy Wales in 2001, Wikipedia, as of this writing, has grown to over 3.5 million articles, contributed by thousands of users worldwide, by employing online collaborative technologies to capture the original writing, vetting, editing, and accumulation of ideas.[2]

Advantages of Creative Collaboration in the Digital World

There are some unique advantages to creating and collaborating in the online digital world. As mentioned above and in previous chapters, we can tap into the co-expertise of diverse participants, we can accumulate and aggregate resources and ideas, and we can share them among the group, or with the public at large. But there are still further advantages to collaborating online that help us innovate and create the new:

The digital tools themselves are plentiful, user-friendly, and economical.
Increasingly, on an almost daily basis, the Internet and its users offer new collaborative tools that can support our work. Many of these tools are free or low-cost, and are designed to be user-friendly.

Whether we are sharing documents through Google, creating multimedia commentary through Voicethread, or touching base with colleagues via Skype, the tools and their functionality continue to expand.

The digital tools are multi-media, multi-sensory, and dynamic.
Decades ago, when the Internet was in its nascent state and primarily used by government agencies and universities, working in a digital environment meant responding to text-based information. Today, images, video, audio, and other forms of multi-media allow us to express ourselves in new ways. From an educational perspective, these diverse forms of media can help us better communicate in ways that connect with our learning styles.[3]

We have almost endless raw materials at our disposal.
As museums and other organizations and individuals continue to contribute more to the shared space of the Internet, we find that we have almost endless materials and resources at our disposal that can support our collaborative work. Whether digital images from museum websites, essays and articles, videos and podcasts, nearly all of these materials are available to the public.

We are using tools and media that ultimately increase our digital literacy, and help us understand how people communicate.
By collaborating online with one another and with our visitors, we are increasing our own digital literacy and learning about how the world is communicating in the 21st century. It is important for museum professionals to stay abreast of the ways our visitors communicate with one another, so that we can literally and figuratively speak their language.

Re-Visiting and Reflecting: Evaluating Our Online Collaboration

Learning is a latent concept, meaning that we can't actually witness learning itself happening. We can only see the evidence of learning through some other means, such as written correspondence, or the creation of a work of art, or through dialogue. Perhaps this final aspect is one of the most important assets that online collaborative learning can offer museums and visitors. By capturing and documenting our online interactions, whether they be threaded discussions, recordings of webinars or Skype chats, or a wiki that we have collaboratively created, technology has the wonderful ability to provide a type of digital mirror that we can examine over time. By using technologies to collaborate, we have new opportunities to examine our practice, and ultimately to provide more evidence for our work and to bolster our cycle of improvement.[4]

For example, by re-visiting our dialogues in online threaded discussions, or watching a recording of a webinar that took place as part of our collaborative work, we have opportunities to re-visit and re-think our work in ways that are rarely possible in the analog world. By examining the digital artifacts of our collaboration, we can easily see the contributions of all involved, where changes were made, and where there is room for improvement. As we plan for future projects and programs, this type of material is invaluable, as it becomes a map or guide for us to examine our experiences and make well-informed choices going forward.

But still further, there is an advantage to online collaborative learning with respect to evaluation: the evaluation process itself can be a collaborative effort, accessed by all involved. Rather than the sometimes teacher-centered or teacher-driven aspect of evaluation, in an online collaborative learning environment each participant has the ability to assess the progress and the success of the process and product. In addition to self-evaluation and peer evaluation, the group of collaborators can thoughtfully examine the process-artifacts of their interaction and make a collective judgment regarding whether or not they have met their goals.

Online collaborative learning, through its ability to document and archive all of our interactions, process-artifacts, and creations, affords new opportunities to become reflective practitioners. While in-person teaching and learning rarely allows for re-examination of each component, online collaborative learning invites us to constantly re-visit and re-examine our creations, not only as individuals, but also as a community.

• • • Case Studies

In the following case studies, we see ways that museums and organizations are using online technologies to solve existing challenges and create new approaches to their educational work. Jessica Hamlin, director of education and public programs for the non-profit organization Art21, describes her experience using online technologies to seek evidence of how teachers are using their resources and materials. In the second case study we hear from museum educators and staff from the American Museum of Natural History and the Metropolitan Museum of Art about their recent collaborative blended teacher program, *Art, Science, and Inquiry*, and the next steps that they will take to share expertise and ideas with museums and teachers in California.

Endnotes

1 A selection of articles about the role of creativity and its expanding definitions in 21st century arts learning can be found in *Art Education, The Journal of the National Art Education Association*, January 2011, Vol. 64, No. 1.

2 For a wonderful discussion of the history of the encyclopedia and also the creation and culture of Wikipedia, see Reagle, Jr., Joseph Michael. *Good Faith Collaboration: The Culture of Wikipedia.* MIT Press, 2010.

3 Gardner, Howard. *Frames of Mind: The Theory of Multiple Intelligences.* Basic Books, 1983.

4 For a discussion of museums and the ongoing cycle of holistic intentionality, see Korn, Randi. "A Case for Holistic Intentionality," *Curator: The Museum Journal,* April 2007.

ART21 AND PROFESSIONAL DEVELOPMENT

By Jessica Hamlin

Art21 is uniquely positioned to work with educators from across the country and around the world. As a non-profit contemporary art organization with a national and increasingly international reach, we illuminate the creative processes of today's visual artists through the production of documentary films, educational resources, professional development and live events. Without an exhibition space or physical collection, we utilize our broadcast capabilities on national public television, a growing internet-based archive, and social networking forums to increase awareness of, access to, and use of contemporary art among broad educational and community-based audiences. Based on our educational mission to increase accessibility to contemporary art and artists, we have realized a larger role in the field of art education: to help bridge the divide between art being made today and art education that often relies on modernist theories centered around skills-based instruction and the elements and principles of design.

While our rich archive of virtual resources and dissemination strategies affords a wide reach, direct contact with audiences has been limited. Collaboration with museums present one means of connecting with audiences through screening events for the general public and professional development for regional educators. Art21 films and online resources contextualize direct experiences with works of art by providing access to the artist's voice and working process.

Art21 has developed a dynamic network of colleagues in museum education and interpretation. Museum partnerships highlight the complementary resources each institution offers. Our collaborations are based on the opportunity to connect objects on view with behind-the-scenes footage that provides insight on how and why these objects were made. Screening events integrate a discussion or hands-on component that addresses museum goals and resources, and is supported by Art21 Screening Guides and discussion prompts provided in free educational materials. Workshops for educators have taken many forms, and are designed to address specific exhibitions, local audiences, and museum interests. Thematic or single-artist exhibitions offer an opportunity to explore content from the Art21 archive and related strategies for introducing to students in the classroom. In some cases workshops look at contemporary art from a broad perspective, exploring questions such as, What makes a work of art a work of art? What materials and tools do artists use today? What are the subjects, issues, and themes important to artists working today? This introduction often prepares participants to focus more effectively on a single artist or thematic exhibition.

Fig. 1: Art21 Professional Development in Museum Galleries

And yet, after several years of offering single and multiple-session workshops in collaboration with individual museums or school districts, we reflected on how little we knew about the impact of our work in the classroom. Feedback forms, focus groups, and other forms of evaluation rendered limited useful information or anecdotes. While workshop participants were required to complete an evaluation, there was a sense of frustration about how difficult follow-up and follow-through was with this professional development format. Working with a limited number of teachers in a finite period of time, with few opportunities to see the results back in the classroom, left us wondering how to understand what we were really able to do in these workshops, and what the outcomes were, once the presentation was over. How does Art21 support the use of contemporary art in the classroom? Are we able to nurture 21st-century teaching strategies inspired by the work of living artists? What are the most effective ways to use video and multimedia resources to engage students?

To advocate effectively for the role of Art21 and contemporary art in classrooms as a powerful teaching tool—a mirror of contemporary society and a window through which students can view and deepen their understanding of the world and themselves—we recognized the need to build long-term relationships with teachers. We needed to think about professional development as an ongoing collaboration that would not just deposit useful information without seeing the results, but would allow us to learn with teachers, and in turn, to present real stories and visual evidence that had the power to inspire others. These aspirations led to the conception of Art21 Educators.

> *"Art21 Educators has greatly impacted how I use technology. I am braver about all manner of technology, from simply using email and sending attachments to using video as a method of critique."*
>
> Jennie Duke, Beacon High School, Beacon, NY

> *"Art21's uniqueness in terms of professional development for teachers lies in the way it builds knowledge, access, and educational relationships to contemporary art and artists."*
>
> Joanne Ross, Glen Rock High School, Glen Rock, NJ

Program Design

Art21 Educators is a year-long professional development initiative designed to support K-12 art and media teachers in their use of contemporary art, artists, ideas, and media in the classroom. The goals of the program are to cultivate a national network of experienced contemporary educators who are able to make connections between contemporary art-making and their own teaching, who produce innovative curricula based on Art21 and other contemporary cultural resources, who successfully use film and online media in the classroom, and who document their classroom experiences and share strategies for effective teaching using contemporary art, artists, and media. In addition, the program was conceived as an opportunity to learn from and with other educators, and to subsequently develop case studies—multi-media narratives written by teachers—that describe the possibilities and real-life experiences inspired by Art21 resources and contemporary art in the classroom.

Our pilot year began in July 2009 with 15 participants from three cities: Los Angeles, Chicago, and New York. Teachers are selected to attend in pairs to help support their work back in the classroom. Often teams apply from the same school or school district, but in several instances, partners have consisted of colleagues living in different cities. Teachers are not required to have any specific technology experience to participate, but must express a willingness to learn about and use new technologies with training provided by Art21. In 2010 we expanded the program to serve teachers nationwide with an emphasis on teachers serving diverse rural, suburban and urban student populations. The program combines live and virtual encounters, as well as synchronous and asynchronous participatory forums.

A six-day summer institute held in New York City sets the stage for the year and introduces key concepts, including connecting contemporary artistic practice with teaching practice, planning curriculum driven by ideas rather than technical skills, and teaching with film and online resources. A full set of Art21 materials, including DVDs, companion books, and Educators' Guides, are given to each participant to bring back to their classrooms and share within their schools and school districts. In addition to introducing a wide range of content to support the development of individual curricula, the institute allows relationships and a sense of community to build in real space and time. This camaraderie then extends into the various virtual forums afterwards. The strong sense of community within the program is reflected in the excitement of all participants who earnestly look forward to opportunities to interact with each other online throughout the year.

Following the institute, monthly online sessions are facilitated in Safari Montage Live!™, an interactive videoconferencing platform where teachers can participate in discussions, lead presentations, and share written, visual, and video materials with each other. Safari Montage Live!™ is used for real-time presentations and discussions intended to support new teaching strategies and to address issues pertinent to their needs and experiences. Additional classroom documentation is shared on a private social networking site hosted by Ning.com. To facilitate documentation, participants are given a FlipCam—a personal video camcorder for self-reflective activities, such as filming their teaching, classrooms, and confessional narratives about the program, as well as to capture student reactions and working methods. Teachers are encouraged to use the camcorders as a tool for teaching—for in-process critiques, student-to-student interviews, and research, planning, and demonstration purposes. Our learning curve was steep during the first year of the program and our progress slow and determined in utilizing these technologies and harnessing them to support effective documentation, sharing and self-reflection.

> *"No other professional development I have participated in attempted to cover much more than classroom management or [the use of] new technology. The institute challenged us to delve below the surface of typical pedagogy, to prod our students toward deep reflection and personal investigation."*
>
> Jennie Duke, Beacon High School, Beacon, NY

> *"The program has really made me think harder about what my students do with the skills that I'm teaching them. How can I encourage them to make meaningful projects, not just rote exercises with predictable results?"*
>
> Troy Kroft, Glen Rock High School, Glen Rock, NJ

Fig. 2: Art21 Educators Using Flip Camera During a Visit at Oliver Herring's Studio

Technology in Practice

Both the Ning site and the online sessions have yielded an enormous archive of classroom documentation. In our pilot year, this flood of documentation was overwhelming and often difficult for participants as well as Art21 to navigate, assess, and react to. However, this content—real teaching experiences directly related to Art21 materials—is invaluable. Not only do we see and hear from the teachers, we can also see how new resources and teaching strategies are influencing classroom dynamics and being interpreted by students in their work. Being able to follow and react to teachers as they try out new strategies and introduce new ideas to their students allows Art21 to nurture and sustain deeper relationships with each of the participants and support their work in real time, as well as inform our thinking about supporting teachers beyond the Art21 Educators network.

Fig. 3: Art21 Educators Ning Home Site

Online collaborative tools like the Ning site and Safari Live!™ also provide open forums for discussing ideas and sharing experiences. The openness of these forums has allowed teachers to feel a sense of ownership and control over the content they are sharing and the narratives they are constructing with the help of their colleagues. In this way, technology has supported a range of different (sometimes even divergent) perspectives and teaching strategies, allowing them to co-exist. In turn, this has shifted expectations away from a single expert or "right way" to do things. The comment function in Ning has supported a rich dialogue between teachers in support of their goals as they react to each other and respond to posted questions and concerns. Ongoing commentary and motivational support among participants encourages teachers to post what they are most proud of, as well as request guidance and advice.

Teacher participation and reflection in the form of blog posts, video footage, and examples of student work provides a constant source of feedback and forces us as facilitators to be nimble with the programmatic design and implementation. As we see things working in particular classrooms, or as we solicit questions or concerns, discussion can quickly shift from an individual context to a full group forum. Our ability to react to teacher feedback and be more responsive to participant needs has allowed teachers to have more ownership in the program and to see their feedback effectively integrated into its design.

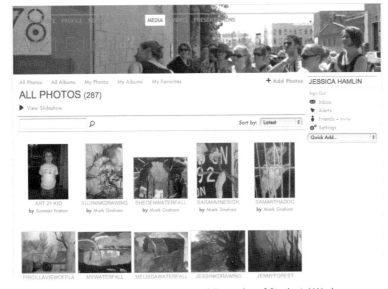

Fig. 4: Art21 Educators Ning Site: Photos and Examples of Students' Work

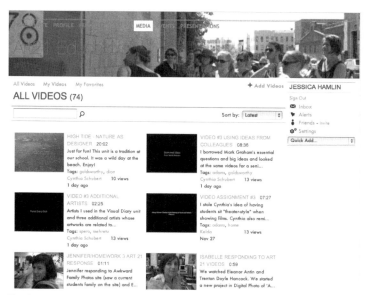

Fig. 5: Art21 Educator Ning Sites: Teacher Uploaded Videos

Although we speculated that a program of this intensity and length might compel some teachers to drop out over the course of the year, the ongoing support and engagement of the community have brought the group closer together. Time management and scheduling issues for busy teachers have forced us to think about how we can organize the year more effectively to manage expectations for participation, but all teachers have sustained their involvement and many return as alum to contribute to the next institute. We are getting a more realistic picture of what teachers are facing in diverse classrooms, including the pressures, hurdles, and limitations. Understanding these real constraints allows us to manage our own expectations and informs us about what we can provide and how we can help, given our goals.

> *"I think the most important part of the online sessions is that we continue to build our relationships with one another. Those relationships give us confidence to post our work and ask others for help or feedback. Hearing everyone's struggles and successes has been helpful. You don't feel alone when you try new things."*
>
> Tanya Manabat, Lawndale Elementary School, Lawndale, CA

"I use the Ning to see what others are doing and to get new ideas for my teaching practices and curriculum. It is fun to share what I am doing with people who are interested because I am passionate about what I teach and enjoy sharing that passion with others."

Casey Carlock, Mary Lyon Elementary School, Chicago, IL

Institutional and Programmatic Learning

The online collaborative tools we use in this initiative have also influenced our own work within the organization. Materials we create for broader educational audiences, including how we think about the content and experience of our web site as well as our published Educators' Guides, are now informed by the experiences of teachers in the Art21 Educators program. In addition, the collaborative forums we utilize with a national group of participants have influenced our ability to work together as a small department within our own institution. Safari Montage Live!™ facilitates meetings with staff who work in and out of the office. In several instances we have developed new ways to facilitate participation in the Art21 Educators Safari Montage Live!™ sessions after utilizing it for administrative purposes.

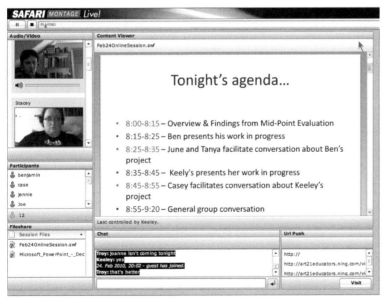

Fig. 6: Art21 Educators Safari Montage Live Session

Fig 7: Art21 Educators Safari Montage Live Session

In addition, Art21 is leveraging these technologies for additional audiences and programmatic efforts, including partnerships with museums to produce new professional development opportunities. In spring 2011 we will present a new workshop series in collaboration with New York's Museum of Modern Art (MoMA) that combines online sessions with an on-site experience in the galleries. This format allows us to model pre-visit and post-visit strategies using Art21 films and MoMA web resources in an online environment. The workshop also includes the opportunity to experience the works of art in person at MoMA. Sessions focus on how teachers can effectively integrate museum field trips into curriculum, with a specific focus on exploring contemporary art. The design of the workshop models three stages for working with students in the context of a museum visit: strategies for preparing students for what they will see, facilitating active participation onsite, and reflecting on and making connections to next steps using related video and online resources. Including virtual components in this workshop also provides more opportunities for teachers to share their own experiences in the classroom, design related curricular materials to share with colleagues, and to follow-up with the group about what happens between and after sessions.

"Integrating technology into our already successful partnership was the next logical step, as it allows us to dovetail our institutional missions with our programmatic goals, as well as allow us to truly model how teachers can easily access all of the digital assets that both MoMA and Art21 have to offer."

Lisa Mazzola, Assistant Director, School and Teacher Programs, The Museum of Modern Art

Technology and the Future of ART21 Educators

For the pilot year of the Art21 Educators program we were very open with participants about our own learning process and desire for them to help us develop the program. We invited our inaugural teachers to be co-producers, to help us refine and revise the program based on our collective experiences and ideas. We attempted to introduce key ideas and content but we were learning with the teachers every step of the way. Our challenge for future years is to maintain that level of flexibility and openness within pre-designed technologies and designated formats. We aspire to use technology in ways that mimic and support the organic and responsive nature of teaching, learning, and making art today—encouraging all participants, including teachers and Art21 staff, to experiment, to play, to question, to think critically and creatively while making meaning in the process.

"Churning over Art21's big ideas with other educators fortified my own art education practices... maybe by simply having a venue to state them, to test my views out on peers."

Lucia Vinograd, Besant Hill School of Happy Valley, Ojai, CA

"I did not anticipate the degree to which technology would influence the program and I am grateful for the learning experience that has provided... I expected to learn a lot from the summer institute, which I certainly did, but did not imagine the way in which the program continues to influence my daily teaching life."

Pam Posey, Crossroads School, Santa Monica, CA

ART, SCIENCE, AND INQUIRY: COLLABORATION AS A MEANS TO EXPLORE INTERDISCIPLINARY INTEGRATION

Introduction

In the fall of 2007, the Metropolitan Museum of Art (MMA) and the American Museum of Natural History (AMNH) began conversations about a collaborative teacher professional development program on the topic of art and science integration. The two institutions had collaborated in the past on one- or two-day teacher workshops, but these new conversations created a spark for a different idea—a longer summer teacher institute that utilized online learning technologies to extend the museum experience, to immerse participants in digital museum resources that could be integrated into the classroom, and to create a space where participants could collaborate and share ideas.

Although staff at both institutions were excited about the possibilities that this type of collaboration could offer, some challenges became clear: How much time would it take to create such a program, and what would our respective roles be? What would be the key themes or focus of the program, and how could we link our institution and our collections in a way that would be meaningful for the teacher-participants? Would we need to bring in additional staff to contribute, perhaps from different departments, or even from outside our institutions? What types of additional resources would be needed—the online tools themselves, or training? And finally, given the amount of time and effort that this collaboration would surely require, how could this program live beyond a three-week period, and how could the participants, and the public at large, continue to benefit?

The two institutions saw this partnership as an exchange and a learning opportunity from the start. Both institutions viewed the collaboration as a means to learn more about best practices in teacher professional development, to explore the new and increasingly dynamic possibilities that online learning could offer, and a way to get to know the individual staff members in both institutions so that we could continue to share ideas beyond this program. Both museums had prior experience offering online or blended learning programs, but in different formats: the American Museum of Natural History's Seminars on Science program has offered graduate-level science courses for teachers using asynchronous threaded conversations and digital resources since 2000, and the Met had explored synchronous webinars and wiki activities for the past year.

The Program and Participants

After several months of meetings, sharing and editing Google documents to outline activities, and lively debates, the program was first offered for 27 teachers in the summer of 2009. By using a linking theme of inquiry, the participants would explore the connections between visual arts and science, and how artists and scientists share similar approaches and thinking skills. The program was three weeks online—asynchronous activities such as blog entries, threaded discussion, and wiki projects, and four live webinars. The program also included two full days of on-site workshops in each institution, so that participants could experience the collections, meet one another, and deepen their conversations.

Below is the syllabus for the initial program that was offered in 2009:

Blended Teacher Institute: Art, Science, and Inquiry
A collaboration between the Metropolitan Museum of Art and the American Museum of Natural History

Orientation Week: July 6-12
- Teachers are invited into the Epsilen workshop
- Teachers set-up their Epsilen E-Porfolios
- Teachers write a blog to introduce themselves and complete pre-program survey
- Pre-workshop activities

Week 1: July 13-19
- Welcome, The Metropolitan Museum of Art
- Close Observation: The Hudson River School
- An Introduction to the Art and Science of Objects Conservation
- A Living Work of Art: Central Park
- Weekend Art Project: Creating a Landscape
- Additional Exploration: Roxy Paine on the Roof
- Contribute to the Activity Wiki

Week 2: July 20-26
- Welcome, American Museum of Natural History
- Case Studies: Scientific Inquiry
- Ongoing Discussions with Educators and Scientists
- Begin Developing a Class Lesson or Activity

Week 3: July 27-31
- On-Site Workshops: Monday, July 27 and Tuesday, July 28
- Writing a Lesson Plan or Classroom Activity to Share with the Group
- Post-workshop discussion and reflection, final blog entries and post-program evaluation

Elluminate Live Webinar Sessions

Session I: Welcome, Overview of Program, Introduction to Close Observation and Inquiry
Monday, July 19, 4-5 pm Eastern Time
During this session, we will introduce ourselves, have an orientation to the program, and begin thinking about close observation and inquiry.

Session II: The Art and Science of Objects Conservation

Wednesday, July 21, 4-5 pm Eastern Time
Join us as we learn about the art and science of objects conservation with Beth Edelstein, an Objects Conservator at the Metropolitan Museum of Art.

Session III: Introduction to the American Museum of Natural History
    Tuesday, July 27, 4-5 pm Eastern Time
    During this session we'll meet staff from the American Museum
       of Natural History and explore more topics that connect with
       inquiry and art and science integration.

Virtual Class Reunion!
    Wednesday, November 17 at 4:30 pm ET
    During this Virtual Class Reunion we will hear how you have incor-
       porated some of the ideas and works of art from this program
       into your teaching. We hope that you will join us!

The following edited conversation was recorded in August, 2009 at the
conclusion of our first summer. During the conversation, some key questions and ideas surfaced, and these informed our future thinking about
the collaboration.

The participants in this conversation are:

- Robert V. Steiner, Ph.D., Director of Online Teacher Education
  Programs, AMNH

- David Randle, Senior Manager of Professional Development, AMNH

- Katie Rasmussen, Manager, *Seminars on Science*, AMNH

- William Crow, Museum Educator, School and Teacher Programs,
  MMA

- Becky Ruderman, Education Programs Associate, MMA

- Alice W. Schwarz, Museum Educator, MMA

- Herminia Din, Associate Professor of Art Education, University of
  Alaska Anchorage

PROGRAM INCEPTION AND PLANNING: WHY COLLABORATE?

Rob Steiner: I'm always interested in what my counterparts are doing
in other places. I had been reaching out to other museums when we first
met, but hadn't reached out to the Met. I wasn't aware of the extent of the
activity there with respect to online learning. After meeting with William,
it was clear that we both had the interest and excitement in the possibility

of collaboration. With our two multi-faceted institutions working together, it was clear that one could potentially create something really remarkable.

William Crow: When we first met for a cup of coffee in the fall of 2007, the Met had just offered our first online/on-site teacher workshop the previous summer. We knew that we wanted to explore that format further to see what the possibilities could be. I think we had also seen how we could bring together diverse participants through using an online platform—learners from different states and even different countries, to examine this topic. It made me wonder what would happen if we started looking outside of ourselves as an institution to find new kinds of expertise. I had heard about the online learning programs at AMNH through a colleague, and we were eager to learn more about the possibilities. I think that at first we struggled during our initial in-person planning meetings—we were trying to figure out what the connecting threads are, besides the more obvious science that's happening at the art museum and art that's happening at the science museum. What do we mean by inquiry? How could that be a continuing conversation in the program? We had to think more about what the big ideas, themes and thinking skills that connect these institutions were, and how we could work outside of our comfort zone.

Dave Randle: The program was a great opportunity to stretch what was happening at both institutions and really combine our resources to create a program that we thought would be very powerful for teachers. It quickly became obvious that we would learn a lot from each other. When we landed on the theme of inquiry, we realized that there were some pretty significant differences in the ways we viewed this topic. At AMNH we have been teaching about scientific inquiry and have some very specific ways that we go about it. In science education, inquiry has been fairly well defined. In broadening our focus to inquiry related to art, we found that it opened up exciting new avenues for exploration and expanded our views of the topic.

Rob Steiner: I think initially what was important was our commitment to using an online learning approach to see how we could deepen the in-person museum experience and bring our institutions together. Starting with a general spirit of goodwill and trust, on both sides I think, we played together with the online environments a little bit, with Epsilen providing us with a common online space for initial exploration. Then later, as we actually began to craft the outline of the course and specific ideas for content and began then to fill in the platform, that shared environment became even more useful. Eventually the online space became a central means of planning, because it facilitated easy access to communication and to the actual course creation. In the later stages it became essential. It was really liberating to know that we could keep making changes to this common space, that we weren't cranking out paper documents or a book that once printed, could not be modified. Instead we could keep working on it until just before the program roll-out.

Katie Rasmussen: Collaboration can be hard. While we were excited to say yes to things, we were also constantly hitting that ceiling of how much we could realistically do. One has to temper the enthusiasm for the collaboration with how much time, staff, and resources it's going to take. I think that the human time component, for collaborations in general, needs to be a big factor.

William Crow: That's true. Finding a way to balance the time that this collaboration required wasn't easy, and to make sure that our other programs received the attention that they needed.

THE PARTICIPANTS: REMEMBERING THE AUDIENCE

William Crow: We weren't exactly sure if our target audience existed, since we were shooting for this in-between zone connecting art and science. I remember wondering if the art teachers would be the primary participants or the science teachers? And what would be the balance between primary and secondary grades, since we kept the program open to all grade levels.

Katie Rasmussen: I think we even talked about encouraging art and science teacher pairs or small groups from the same district, school, or area to apply together.

Rob Steiner: I had a concern that we were investing a great deal of time in this collaboration, and we weren't sure that we would actually have participants enroll.

Becky Ruderman: I was concerned about it, too. Actually seeing the applications coming in very slowly at first made me wonder how we were going to drum up more interest. Then all of a sudden there were these third parties interested in the program, like the Green Magnet School in Queens that ended up sending six teachers, and then the New York City Garden Club contacted us to offer scholarships to sponsor six teachers.

Katie Rasmussen: At AMNH we offered other New York City professional development credit courses that occasionally ended up not running, due to lack of enrollments. They were also blended, three weeks online with a day here at the museum, but I think the combination of this program being something new and interesting and also really being applicable to all teachers, sort of cross-disciplinary, made it a success in terms of enrollment. The fact that it is about both art and science means that other teachers who might not fit in to either of these disciplines also feel comfortable applying, because the blending of disciplines makes it clear that you don't have to know everything about each content area. Part of our issue was realizing that we could always do a program that talks about art in science and science in art and have people be interested. But if you're going to have a group of teachers take a three-week course, there must be something that's really applicable to what their school, district, and summer vacation requirements are. In the end, our central topic of "inquiry" is something that all teachers need to understand and know how to utilize in the classroom, no matter their subject or grade level. Using a central topic of inquiry gave us focus, and it gave the teachers focus.

THE BLENDED FORMAT: ONSITE AND ONLINE

Katie Rasmussen: I think that the blended format is a wonderful aspect of this program. Between the two institutions, and the multiple forms of interaction online and in-person, there's really something to interest every style of learner. Someone who might be intimidated to contribute something in-person might be able to better express themselves in a blog format, and vice versa.

Alice Schwarz: We see the same kind of thing in school visits, when a teacher will say, "Robbie never speaks in class, but the whole time he was in the gallery with you he spoke out." I think it comes down to different learning styles and different comfort levels with the subject and the situation.

Dave Randle: I agree. We see this at AMNH as well. In some cases I think it has really turned around teacher/student relationships because the teacher gets a new view of certain kids.

Herminia Din: It seems like we're all used to teaching face-to-face, and this is kind of online approach shifting the paradigm of how we teach. In the face-to-face environment, we are familiar with all kinds of learning situations and know how to make that connection with our audiences. In a 100% online environment, it can be different. But in this hybrid environment there are so many new things for us to experiment with that I think it will just take a little more time to play around and draw new connections.

Alice Schwarz: But I also think that the participants divide their learning styles very much between the two components, and interact in different ways both online and in-person. There's a type of participation you do at home by yourself, and a type that you do in a group with an instructor. I think we all conduct ourselves differently in each situation. I think our generation in particular still sees a great behavioral separation between the two components.

Katie Rasmussen: I've been using online tools since I was in grade school, truthfully. So it may be something that feels more natural to me. No matter what your background, though, there are always just going to be some people that are more comfortable participating in an online environment, and others in an in-person environment.

Becky Ruderman: During the two on-site days, the participants were really excited just to see one another face to face. When I handed out all of their nametags they were just so excited to match everyone with their name.

Alice Schwarz: Speaking of the on-site days, I'm wondering if there's a way we could have made more of an effort to concretely bring what they did online to the in-person sessions?

William Crow: I think it's probably one of the next big challenges of blended learning experiences—to make use of the information and activities from the online experiences and make stronger connections with the on-site component.

Alice Schwarz: Another question is, is it okay to leave the online and on-site parts as disparate experiences?

Dave Randle: I think that we could have made a stronger connection between the on-site and online components. It was partly a case of having too many really cool things to show at each institution. That said, I think we were successful in using the on-site days to wrap up the ideas we were working with online. This was brought home when we read evaluation comments from some of the folks who were out of state and not able to make it to the face-to-face days. They complained that the online part of the course lacked closure. We didn't get comments like these from anyone who was at the two onsite days. I think we were able to do some wrap-up and connect the ideas we were grappling with during the previous two weeks.

Katie Rasmussen: When you have a group onsite, you want to make sure to build in time for quiet personal reflection, but you can only do so much of that because you have them for such a limited time and you want to maximize discussion. Sometimes there are other, more pressing goals to accomplish. One of the nicest things about having the online component before and after is, it gives you a dedicated time and place to be reflective without cutting in to your time onsite.

Rob Steiner: I think that this blended format has enormous potential to create a powerful opportunity for unique experiences for teachers and students within a museum. We can provide strong online preparation in advance of the in-person museum sessions, which means that the level of questioning and dialogue at those in-person sessions may be deeper and more sophisticated than it would otherwise be. We all know how hard it is to actually get a group of people into any place for several hours, and so, once having gotten them there, we certainly want to make the most of those hours. This format provides an opportunity to do that.

WHAT DID WE LEARN?

Katie Rasmussen: You know, I was thinking about what some of the teachers were saying yesterday and today during the on-site workshops, about observing museum professionals in two different fields, one science and one art, working so well together and learning from each other. To me it's about continuing collaborations like this and bringing institutions together, not only because we learn so much from each other, but because we set the collaborative example for teachers. Some of those art teachers and science teachers are going to go back to their schools and think, "You know what? I can call Sally down the hall, who teaches art, because I've got this nifty new activity to do between my science class and her art class." Because they see institutions thinking collaboratively, they realize individuals and schools could do it, too.

Rob Steiner: This collaboration allowed me to explore areas that were not necessarily a primary focus of our AMNH online offerings. One big motivation to do this collaboration was to learn from the Met's greater experience in conducting live webinars. In addition, the platform incorporated a number of Web 2.0 features that, again, were not a central focus of our own programs, and so this was another great learning opportunity for us. The other thing that became very clear to me is that Will and his colleagues were very well prepared, organized, and meticulous—and both AMNH and the Met agreed that generous planning time was important to maximize the prospects of success in this relatively complicated endeavor. We gave ourselves nearly a year, off and on, to do the planning, and that was really helpful. With a set of topics as complex as this, rushing could have been really messy.

Katie Rasmussen: I think that one of the joys of an online course is its ability to be replicated in the future. Obviously you improve, you switch pieces in and out, but that basic framework of a course is there and can be repeated in some form. Building a course from scratch takes a really long time. The work that we've already completed becomes both a course that's ready to go, and also a fresh slate where you can go in and make those changes as our thinking changes.

Rob Steiner: Ultimately, any collaboration needs to support the respective institutional missions. And the choice of partners and projects needs to be informed by strategic considerations, as well as practical considerations such as staff time. There is ultimately a balancing act of deciding, given your staff and resources, the likely future value of present collaboration. So there is an element of risk – things may or may not pan out in large or smaller ways. Despite many discussions with many organizations, relatively few discussions about potential collaboration lead to actual collaboration. In my own experience, I would guess that about 95% of the time, nothing very substantial transpires. But that other 5% can be very important, and I hope that our current work is in that 5%. So there is a balancing act, and sometimes you have to learn to say no, that it sounds really interesting but we just don't think we can do it right now. The reward of this collaboration was the very intense satisfaction that I felt at the end of the day that we had done something genuinely new and wonderful. And the optimism that some of this may actually translate back in the classrooms is very gratifying. For me, I think some of the lessons are that collaboration is possible with the right partners and the right purpose. Our institutions may have had different motivations, but there was a distinctive advantage for each in going forward with this. I think, as an aside, that while it may not be strictly essential, it helps enormously if you like and respect your collaborators. I always looked forward to our meetings. We had a sense of confidence and trust in one another. An example of the impact of this experiment is that we are now going to talk to our Public Programs division about the possibility of collaborating with them to institute a regular set of webinars. While we have done isolated webinars for the National Science Teachers Association and others, our experience with the preparation and participation in the four live webinars of this program was central in providing me with the confidence that AMNH can go forward and provide such experiences on a regular basis in very different contexts.

Alice Schwarz: For me it was also the excitement of trying something new. Then it was the thrill of getting to be a student at the American Museum of Natural History. It was such a pleasure to remind myself that learning doesn't end even if you're an educator. It motivates me to reciprocate in our galleries. As a museum educator it's nice to be constantly reminded what it's like to be a student.

Katie Rasmussen: I think in some ways this collaboration was profession-al development for us. I also want to mention that one of the key pieces to a successful partnership like ours is finding a partner where you not only have that same keen interest and enthusiasm, but where one partner isn't doing more work than the other. Certainly the trust and accountability can also be a motivating factor in keeping up with each other. When we saw what the Met was doing in constructing the online activities, it moti-vated us to put in our share. It was a positive type of encouragement.

William Crow: We pushed each other in a positive way.

Herminia Din: It's hard for me to envision a collaboration happening without actually being present and wanting to start something new. I think that it takes an initial step—a personal connection—to get a success-ful collaboration started.

Dave Randle: It was great to explore different types of online teaching tools. In our courses we haven't done a lot with real time interaction yet. It was interesting to see how the webinars fit in. We also haven't used the kind of group collaboration tools that Epsilen has built into it. It was particularly interesting for me to watch the teachers collaborating on the case study in their group wikis.

Next Steps: Art and Science Integration from Coast to Coast, a Four-Institution Collaboration

During the summer of 2010 we offered the program *Art, Science, and Inquiry* again, for 29 teachers. We made some adjustments to the program based on teacher feedback, including an in-person orientation session at the start of the three-week program. We also made the decision to further streamline our activities to give the program even more focus, and to make clearer connections between art and science using the lens of inquiry.

Also during the summer of 2010, we were joined by colleagues from the California Academy of Sciences and de Young, the Fine Arts Museum of San Francisco. These two institutions have been offering art and science integration programs for students for the past several years, and we were eager to learn from one another. Helena Carmena, Manager of Teacher Services at the California Academy of Sciences, and Emily Jennings, Museum Educator from the de Young Museum, both observed and participated in the online sessions, and Helena was able to travel to New York City for the two on-site days and provide an hour-long guest workshop with the teachers.

Through these observations and conversations it has become clear that there is much we can learn from one another. The California museums have developed a range of on-site activities and lessons that authentically integrate art and science, with a focus on 21st-century skills, such as critical thinking and creativity. They have experience offering these programs directly with students, have made great strides in finding ways to evaluate the outcomes, and have also found rich partnerships with the San Francisco Unified School District. These two California institutions are eager to explore the possibilities that online learning can offer, and so they are looking to our existing model to explore possibilities. Thus, in the summer of 2011 we plan to offer a four-institution, blended collaborative teacher program, *Integrating Art and Science*, using a combined and co-developed set of activities and lessons for teachers in both New York and San Francisco, and using an online learning environment for the participants to share lessons and expertise.

CONCLUSION

We see a constant and pervasive shift in our daily lives, an evolution from an information-based, compartmentalized culture to one that is increasingly collaborative and interconnected. This change is widespread and it envelopes our lives, at work and at home. From our daily digests of news and social media to the new collective ways in which we purchase commodities, we now have instant access to information, to other people, and to institutions. As we find ourselves located in a shared, global space, our attention has turned now not just to what we access and what we share, but to what we do and how we work together.

As museums define their position within this new global digital context, they need to address their online presence, and also their online interaction with their many publics, as well as with their fellow institutions. As technology allows both museums and their visitors to experience collections in new and innovative ways, museum should be leaders in developing new approaches to these interactions, and see these opportunities as a means to evolve from teaching institutions to learning institutions. Museum educators, curators, conservators, and staff from a wide range of museum departments should see themselves as stakeholders in these new opportunities, and bring their own expertise to the conversation.

Given the constant changes in our culture due to increasingly dynamic and collaborative technologies, a museum's first steps into this terrain may seem risky—and in some ways, they are. As museums already know, the very nature of entering into a collaborative relationship means we must embrace the new and unknown and be willing to accept the results. This attitude and approach may not be natural for some institutions, especially ones that are more comfortable working as autonomous, enclosed units. But no longer can museums see themselves as operating on an island. Our visitors increasingly expect a seamless experience between their online and in-person lives, and with their peers, families and friends.

By starting small, and by involving a few like-minded people with the enthusiasm and energy for the possibilities, museums can find great rewards in the field of online collaborative learning. These rewards include new ways of creating and sharing content, transparent interactions between museum staff and visitors that can be re-visited and re-evaluated, and an opportunity to reflect and learn from our own educational practice. New tools and online platforms allow us to tap our ever-expanding online resources. We, in turn, are able to allow our visitors access to these digital resources, and help them learn how to use these resources for new and creative purposes.

Each institution should consider the path that is best suited for its own situation, goals, and mission. We hope that museums consider the rich possibilities that online collaborative learning can offer, while being aware of the resources and time it requires, and the new challenges it can present. We believe that online collaborative learning, combined with a spirit of sharing, and building upon existing best practices in museum learning, offers great potential for museums to increase their public value.

AUTHORS

WILLIAM B. CROW
Museum Educator
The Metropolitan Museum of Art

William Crow oversees programs for K-12 schools and teachers at The Metropolitan Museum of Art in New York City. Before his work at the Metropolitan, he was a high school teacher at Delbarton School (NJ) and a lecturer at the Morgan Library and Museum. As a practicing visual artist, Crow has exhibited his work extensively in New York City, nationally, and internationally, and his art is represented in both museums and private collections. He is an adjunct instructor of Museum Studies in the graduate faculty of Johns Hopkins University, and a part-time Assistant Professor of Media Studies at The New School, New York. Frequently a presenter at national museum conferences, Crow has also spoken internationally on the topic of museums, education, and media, including recent keynotes and panel discussions in Buenos Aires, Madrid, and Ottawa. In 2009 he co-authored *Unbound by Place or Time: Museums and Online Learning* (The AAM Press). He holds a BA from Wake Forest, an MFA from Hunter College of The City University of New York, and an MSEd in Leadership in Museum Education from Bank Street College. He is currently a PhD student in Cognitive Studies in Education and Intelligent Technologies at Columbia University.

HERMINIA WEI-HSIN DIN, PH.D.
Associate Professor of Art Education
Department of Art
University of Alaska Anchorage

Herminia Wei-Hsin Din is associate professor of art education at University of Alaska, Anchorage. Previously she was the Web Producer at the Children's Museum of Indianapolis and Education Technologist at the Indianapolis Museum of Art. In 2005, she facilitated a docent-training program using the Internet2 videoconferencing method for a traveling exhibition in Alaska, and partnered with University of Alaska Museum of the North to develop the *LearnAlaska* project. Currently she is collaborating with colleagues at the Metropolitan Museum of Art and American Museum of Natural History to offer professional development programs for teachers focusing on art and science integration. She has been a board member of the AAM Media and Technology committee, and served as the MUSE Awards Chair. She was co-editor of *The Digital Museum: A Think Guide* (2007) and co-author of *Unbound by Place or Time: Museums and Online Learning* (2009), both published by The AAM Press. She specializes in distance and online learning for museums, and presents regularly on museum and technology at national and international conferences. She holds a doctorate in art education from Ohio State University.

INDEX

A

access, 75

accreditation, 25n.8

active participation, 76

Adams, Marianna, 65

adjourning, 75

advocacy, 100, 101

American Museum of Natural
History (AMNH), 10–12, 110,
123–135

Ancelet, Jeanine, 99, 100

Anders, William, 9

Anderson, Chris, 18

Apollo 8, 9

apps, 60

archaeology collections, online,
16–17

Art21, 110, 111–121
constraints, 118
Educators, 113–114, 116, 121
future, 121
institutional and programmatic
learning, 119–121
program design, 113–116
technology and the future, 121
technology in practice, 116–119

arts integration, 97

Art, Science, and Inquiry, 110,
123–135

audience, 128–129
future, 134–135
lessons learned, 132–134
onsite-online format, 129–131
program and participants,
124–126

program inception, planning, and
rationale, 126–128

asynchronous tools, 58–59

attendance, 64

audience, 17, 18, 65, 70–71, 99–100,
128–129

B

Balboa Park Cultural Partnership,
63–71

participants, 65

Balboa Park Learning Institute, 60,
63–71

blended format, 129–131

blended learning, 2, 33

blogs, 30, 59

building something new, 105–135
case studies, 110–135

buy-in, 74

C

California Academy of Sciences, 39,
41–51

call-and-response format, 30

Carmena, Helena, 39, 41–51

cell phones, 60

chat, online, 59

climate for learning, 75

co-experts, 77–78

cognition, situated and distributed,
37–38

cognitive theory, 35–37

Collaboration Age, 6

INVEST in YOURSELF

"I want to be the very best in my field and these resources will provide me with the information I need to kick-start my professional development."

Patricia Counihan, Concord Museum, MA

AAM membership gives you access to information for success in your job and career.

- Year-round professional development opportunities
- Timely updates on what's happening in the field
- Online library with thousands of indispensable resources
- Connections to professional networks
- Resources on standards and best practices
- Discounts in the AAM Bookstore
- Alerts to job opportunities and fellowships

Join today!
www.aam-us.org/joinus or 866-226-2150

AMERICAN ASSOCIATION OF MUSEUMS